When Their Behavior is Like a Picture, It Can Never be Mislead, Mistaken, or MisUnderstood

U.S. Constitution Law and the State of North Carolina Law, Rockingham County Judicial Center, Reidsville, North Carolina

True Crime Stories: Investigations & Reports City of Reidsville, Reidsville Police Department, Reidsville, North Carolina

When you're ignored in Private, Speak in Public.

## PREFACE
## That Is The Question

The First & Fourteenth Amendments of the United States Constitution There are exceptions to this rule where the Court finds that governmental interests in disclosure/registration outweigh interference with First Amendment rights. The government may also, generally, not compel individuals to express themselves, hold certain beliefs, or belong to particular associations or groups.

The right to petition the government for a redress of grievances guarantees people the right to ask the government to provide relief for a wrong through the courts (litigation) or other governmental action.

It works with the right of assembly by allowing people to join together and seek change from the government.

Amendment I Congress shall make no law respecting an establishment of religion, or prohibiting the free exercise thereof; or abridging the freedom of speech, or of the press; or the right of the people peaceably to assemble, and to petition the Government for a redress of grievances.

Amendment IV The right of the people to be secure in their persons, houses, papers, and effects, against unreasonable searches and seizures, shall not be violated. No Warrants shall be issued, but upon probable cause, supported by Oath or affirmation, and particularly describing the place to be searched and the persons or things to be seized.

Amendment VIII Excessive bail shall not be required, nor excessive fines imposed, nor cruel and unusual punishments inflicted.

Amendment XIV granted citizenship and equal civil and legal rights to African Americans and enslaved people who had been emancipated after the American Civil War. North Carolina Defamation Law:

Generally speaking, there are two types of defamation in North Carolina: Libel - False statements in written or graphic form, and Slander - False statements in spoken form; 1 For a defamation claim to be viable, essential elements must be proven: That the statement is defamatory, was false, was published or spoken to some other person or third party; That the statement is In some circumstances, that you have suffered actual damages; and, in some circumstances, that the defendant published the falsity with actual malice.

Your name and reputation are essential to you. Depending on your profession, your reputation may be one of your most valuable assets. If someone makes a false and defamatory statement about you to others, it can seriously damage you at work and in your personal life.

You can be physically and emotionally injured, and in today's world, possibly permanently. It can impact your relationships with your friends and family. You may even suffer loss of earnings, capacity to earn, and other economic damages. What You Are About to Read Is True. The names weren't changed to protect the innocent.

I don't care about hearing the aftermath when these readings are finished. But when you're left with no choice, your back is against the wall. Your following adjective is to do what's best for you and yours. For reference, the names included in any literature are also recorded with either the Rockingham County Clerk of Superior Court or North Carolina Middle District Court, along with the names, dates, places, and times of some incidents.

When telling my story, I will do my best to respect the thoughts or feelings of others. But the one thing

I will not do is change my story. It's mine, and I'm the editor of this story.

## INTRODUCTION

### Title VI of the Civil Rights Act of 1964 and the "OJP Program Statute" "Police Misconduct Provision"

Title VI and the OJP (Office of Justice Programs) cover misconduct. Program statute includes, for example, harassment or use of racial slurs, discriminatory arrest, discriminatory traffic stops, coercive sexual conduct, retaliation for filing a complaint with the DOJ or participating in the investigation, discriminatory use of force, or refusal by the agency to respond to complaints alleging discriminatory treatment by its officers.

This Law makes it unfair for state and local law enforcement officers to engage in a pattern or practice of conduct that deprives a person of rights protected by the Constitution or laws of the United States. (34 U.S.C. § 12601).

This law covers conduct such as excessive force, discriminatory harassment, false arrests, coercive sexual conduct, and unlawful stops, searches, or arrests. However, unlike the other civil laws discussed below, the DOJ does not have to prove that discrimination has occurred to prove a pattern or practice of misconduct.

Malicious prosecution claims are filed when a police officer initiates a criminal proceeding without reasonable proof that a crime has been committed. This type of criminal proceeding generally results in the victim. This type of claim protects against emotional stress, embarrassment, and financial expenses that may arise when a criminal case lacks merit.

Ashley Britt is the victim of a "pattern or practice" conducted by Officers C. Bailey & G. Boone. Destiny Pointer, a member of the same household, received a citation from Officer G. Boone. D. Pointer-girlfriend of A—Britt's brother. Latoye Britt, also a member of the same household, received a citation from Officer C. Bailey, charges of DWLR- L. Britt was NOT driving to be charged with DWLR. RPD officers did NOT detain L. Britt.

L Britt was brought to the scene by another child. L. Britt Two daughters and an officer greeted L. Britt in street clothing with a dog tag showing his badge in the rear parking lot.

As I arrived, I spoke with the officer about the safe in the trunk, which was the first reason I was given why she was stopped. The issue was the darkness of the tint. According to the DOJ, the actions of these two officers are concerns for case filing for Pattern "or" Practice in regards to A. Britt. I have enclosed footage of this traffic stop recorded by KFC employees on the night of the incident.

I have been falsely accused and arrested, called and failed by a judge and FTA, and posted bail, all due to Officer Bailey NOT following RPD guidelines and procedures for a traffic stop—public Humiliation. I haven't been in trouble in over five years.

Just by coincidence, another individual falsely accused me of a crime (I have evidence to support my defense of this crime). I have been falsely arrested in my opinion of both cases due to supporting justified documents I have in my possession containing evidence of where I've-we've been a victim/victim of Misconduct of Law Enforcement.

**Preface**

**Introduction**

**Chapter 1**　　　　　**Reidsville Police Department**

**Chapter 2**　　　　　　　　**The Complaint I**

| | |
|---|---|
| Chapter 3 | NC Middle District Court |
| Chapter 4 | The Complaint II |
| Chapter 5 | The Amended Complaint |
| Chapter 6 | Caswell County Sheriff Office I |
| Chapter 7 | Caswell County Sheriff Office II |

## Chapter 1
### September 20, 2022

May 10, 2023, I have provided citation information for all traffic violations in question. In filing this complaint, I have mailed copies of this information to the Mayor of Reidsville, the Chief of Police, the DOJ, the FBI, the SBI, and the NAACP regarding the actions and activities performed by two officers of the Reidsville Police Department. Traffic stops and violations with one individual and two family members of this same individual. Below, we will describe how we feel as we're violated in terms of civil rights, discrimination against, false arrest, the defamation of our character, misconduct of law Enforcement (RPD), and several other violations. You received the following events on September 20, 2022, between Ashley Britt and the RPD.

I have also enclosed the following information to show that my claims for Law Enforcement Misconduct against the RPD are valid. As you read below, this situation began with Ashley Britt and ended with Latoye's Britt mother.

On August 17, 2022, I purchased a 2004 Mercedes Benz, white. The types of medications prescribed for both parties involved being directly in the sunlight or having too much exposure to sunlight, which could cause effects and reactions to the medicines. Tint was placed on all vehicle windows, including the front windshield. According to NC DMV guidelines, We understand that tinting wasn't for the traffic stop. The traffic violation consists of officers C. Bailey (#10176) & G. Boone (10347) of the Reidsville Police Department. During this traffic violation, it's believed Officer Bailey of RPD was staking out the whereabouts and locations of A. Britt.

A. Britt was conversing with a family member in the parking lot of Two Brothers Mini Mart located on Harrison Street, Reidsville. As she was sitting and holding this conversation, she observed Officer Bailey heading toward Lawsonville Avenue under the traffic light. As A. Britt finished her conversation, she drove off, heading toward the corner of Harrison & Way Street, in the opposite direction. After crossing under the traffic light, Officer Bailey rushed upon A. Britt's vehicle as he turned the lights on to signal for her to stop.

This traffic violation took place in the rear parking lot of KFC. Officer Bailey said his reason for the stop was due to tint violations. Officer Bailey called for Boone to assist with the traffic violation because Bailey did not have a tint reader in his possession. Officer Boone responded to the call, once Boone arrived on the scene he demanded Bailey to call the K-9 unit to assist with the traffic violation. * with no understanding of why K-9 was dispatched for a tint violation in the beginning by G. Boone*

See video: contains footage of the actual stop recorded by KFC employees After watching this video gives a better understanding of what happened. Now as to how I became involved, when Officer Bailey rushed in on the vehicle, then approaching the vehicle, it seems to me he did NOT ask for license & registration when he first approached the car, it seem to me Officer Bailey recorded the information he was given by NC DMV when he ran the plates after the fact. At least, these are my thoughts on how I came to have a charge of DWLR from Officer Bailey.

Two of her sisters were on the scene, explaining to officers that the safe in the trunk contained family money that had been saved for family trips. As I arrived on the scene, the same questions asked of her two sisters were the same for myself. I also explained to them that this was family money; we all saved and put our money together for trips and things of that nature.

Officers, he did NOT release the vehicle. He wanted to put the keys in the owner's hand. During this traffic violation, A. Britt was found to have one (1) cocaine crack rock. Later, she was indicted for selling due to the amount of money located in the trunk during the stop. Once I spoke with the officers about the money, it was released to me along with the vehicle upon showing proper identification.

Britt had already been transported by RPD for booking by the time I arrived, and I was able to speak with someone I believed to be a K-9 officer. A. Britt was taken to RCSO for booking, bonding, and processing, on 09/20/22 by Officer Bailey. Officer Bailey presented RCSO Magistrate Jeffery Strader documents for citation number 1J24930. Magistrate Jeffery Strader was given a citation for DWLR. Magistrate J. Strader made Officer Bailey aware of the mistake that had taken place. Magistrate J. Strader and Officer Bailey became distributive with one another. Officer Bailey wrote a citation for the wrong individual during this traffic stop.

Officer Bailey presented those incorrect documents as the arresting documents for A. Britt. Magistrate J. Strader & Officer Bailey disagreed because the incorrect documents were in the wrong individual's name. While attempting to get A. Britt processed, Officer Bailey had to re-do his previous arrest warrant. Once the paperwork was changed and completed at the RCSO in the magistrate office from A. Brit to L. Britt.

Britt was given a bond of $5k once Officer Bailey corrected all paperwork. The correct citation number given to A. Britt afterwards is 1J24931, given to her by Officer Bailey at the magistrate office located in Worth, NC. It's during this time that G. Boone makes racial remarks directed toward my hair texture, stating that "my hair was NOT my hair," indeed that my hair was not real, that it was weed. Britt was asked several times to shake her hair/head by Officer Boone.

Officer Boone replied to say A. Britt's hair was weed, not her hair. On May 5, 2023, I called RCSO to inquire about a warrant for my arrest due to previously being assaulted by an employee of

Dollar General. The communications officer informed me I had two warrants for my arrest. When I asked what the two warrants were, I was told they were simple assault and DWLR. I questioned the date about the DWLR citation; in September, I had a valid, active license.

I renewed my license on 09/28/2022. After learning of this citation, I started researching the traffic violations of these two officers. Officers G. Boone and C. Bailey have combined two traffic violation reports for A. Britt.

Four out of eight traffic violations involved these two officers. During another traffic violation where I was the passenger, on 09/19/2022. We (son's girlfriend & myself) saw Officer Boone as we were topping Morehead Street. Officer Boone proceeded to make a right turn at the intersection of Branch and Morehead street, made a left turn leading to the end of Pennsylvania Avenue, and made another right turn placing him back on Morehead street headed toward the RPD.

We made a right turn in the direction of Lawsonville Avenue, as we passed the old nursing home, Officer Boone turned on the blue lights, we proceeded to pull over to the right of the street. Officer Boone approached our vehicle, asked "if she knew why he stopped her", " the percentage of her tint was illegal." Asked for lic & reg went to his vehicle, came to our measured tint, informed Pointer of a WFA. Pointer did NOT know. He explained the process for both incidents in detail to Pointer.

Also informI informed Pointer of how he was to arrest her for WFA but he was, NOT. The DOB was the wrong pants and he knew it was wrong, she was the right person. We as a family feel we have been violated more than once. With these issues at hand the safety, and welfare of my children is definitely very important to our family.

The actions of these officers may seem small in the eyes of the law, but in the eyes of the public-especially the African-American community, we don't feel safe. These types of situations continue to occur within our communities with our local Law Enforcement. I haven't gotten over the natural death of my parents, ten and one years later. It's devastating for sure, ongoing pain and I surely do NOT want to be that parent standing at the podium asking the community for justice, because of an unjustified killing of an African-American.

Defendants Citation Date Citation No. Officer Officer Badge No Location Vehicle Destiny Pointer 09/19/2022 0J75975 G. Boone 10347 Branch Street

Toyota Ashley Britt 09/20/2022 1J24931 C. Bailey 10176 KFC rear parking Benz Ashley Britt j835018 G. Boone 10347 Freeway Dr BMW Ashley Britt 02/11/2023 3J18455 C. Bailey 10176 Cr. Cypress Dr Honda Latoye Britt 09/20/2022 1J24930 C. Bailey 10176 KFC rear parking n/a In February of 2023, Officer C. Bailey had once again given A. Britt a citation.

This citation was for no operator's license. Officer Bailey advised A. Britt said that he was only going to give her a citation for no operator's license because "she had never given them no problems." Officer Bailey did NOT display the same reactions as he once did on 09/20/2022, when he called for Officer G. Boone to assist with a tint violation. Why the different display of attitudes with each traffic stop?

Reidsville Police Dept. Traffic Stop Violations RPD Officers C. Bailey & G. Boone RPD Badge No. 10176 & 10347 Reason for our complaints: ~ Biased-based policing (race, color, religion, sex, handicap, familial status or national origin) ~ Use of excessive force ~ Rude or discourteous behavior ~ Other (explain) ➢ Officer C. Bailey & Officer G. Boone ➢ Reidsville Police Department Officers-pattern "or" practice ➢ Why was A. Britt was blocked in by an RPD patrol car in the rear parking lot of KFC ➤ Why did Officer Bailey zoom in on her car after she'd finished talking with relatives at the store, Officer Bailey, when asked what prompted the stop, his reply was she was stopped for tint violation.

A. Brit was never given a citation or ticket for the stop and the excuse for the stop given was NOT what you to start with? ➤ Why did Officer G. Boone has Officer C. Bailey called for the K-9 unit during this traffic stop, when he was called to assist with tinting issues? ➤ Why was the K-9 unit needed? ➤ What was the cause for K-9?

Just because she have a previous charge of drugs does NOT give you the right to harass her ■ Just because she was in a drug related area, does that mean she's automatically selling Drugs? ➤ RCSO Magistrate J. Strader-failure to intervene, knowledge of first given incorrect documents by Officer Bailey ➤ Why was it justified by the magistrate of the officer's incorrect documents for the person he was arresting? ➤ Once Officer Bailey was made aware of his mistake, completing a citation in another person's name, why wasn't this taken care of? ➤ Why did Officer Bailey NOT fix his mistake? didn't he fix this situation? ➤ False arrest for this citation-secured bond set by a judge of $1K.

Conclusion: As we have become aware of the Misconduct of Law Enforcement, about two Reidsville Police Officers and another complaint filed against the Sheriff of Caswell County Tony Durden & Chief Major O. Foster for similar pattern "or" practices. The fact that personally my children's lives are a big concern and may be in danger due to the actions shown from Officer C. Bailey & Officer G. Boone of the Reidsville Police Department, badge numbers 10176 & 10347.

I will NOT speak details for the other complaint, just needed to secure my findings. Both officers, we believe, did NOT follow the guidelines set forward by the state of North Carolina, required during traffic violations. Neither officer asked for license and registration for these traffic stops, except for one-with Destiny Pointer. But Officer Boone's reasons for starting the traffic stop. Seems unreliable-had something more to do with tint. Furthermore because both these officers FAILED to identify the person in question. Assuming registration of the vehicles were in A. Britt's name. Also both officers FAILED to cross-check NC DMV driving status available during traffic stops. Each one of the vehicles in question had/have active insurance coverage, each one of the vehicles was registered to a license driver, with one of those licensed drivers being from Danville, VA.

The vehicles involved include, Toyota Camry-D. Pointer, Honda Accord-va licensed driver, 745 BMW-nc licensed driver, Mercedes Benz-L. Britt. Providing this information, and with all vehicles complying with NC DMV guidelines, what were Officers Bailey & Boone probable cause for stopping any of these vehicles. Especially traffic citations received on 2/11/23, A. Britt had just picked up food, returning, when being pulled by Officer Bailey.

Why was A. Britt pulled? What was the probable cause? If Officers Bailey and Boone, I personally feel would've followed procedure. A procedure they were trained to do in a police academy upon a traffic stop was to ask for license and registration. Since Officer Bailey FAILED to do his job, his actions resulted in L. Britt had a FTA for DWLR citation written by Officer Bailey on 09/20/23, (for change of date per Officer Boone, citation 09/21/23, for A. Britt). Unaware of my knowledge of the FTA. Posting bail money for a citation I was NOT reliable for in the beginning. Which leads to false arrest, a violation of my Civil Rights, Defamation of Character, Emotional & Mental stress, increased anxiety.

I learned of this incident because of another legal situation. Officer Bailey did not even have the decency to go back and correct his mistake after being coiled by the magistrate for the wrong documents presented to him. Some other important factors involving this matter are that I was restricted from driving per my physician's orders. On March 22, I had a self-involved accident, causing damage to real property.

The DA dismissed this citation in admin court, I provided the necessary documentation from the owners where they were NOT going to pursue legal actions against me. The DA dismissed my case. This citation involved state highway patrol & RCSO. A few months later I received a speeding ticket on highway business 29, from a state highway patrol my license WAS indeed suspended for this speeding ticket. NC DMV did take my license for 30 days, my privileges were restored, I needed to pay the fine. Also with this citation, I appeared in admin court, the DA was NOT comfortable reducing the speed herself, so she asked another DA in district court to approve her decision. Returning to court, I was given a fine with time to pay, with sending on/2022.

My license is still suspended due to non-payment of the restoration fee and the speeding ticket. I've just chosen not to pay, as I'm restricted from driving. If I pay the ticket, I will drive. So yes, I know my license is now suspended, but it's through my choice, not the NC DMV. I have not been stopped for traffic violations by a Reidsville Police Officer. My last two encounters with law enforcement were conducted with the NC State Highway Patrol.

Thank you for allowing me to express my concerns and thoughts of these two individuals who took an oath to protect and serve. Their actions are unjustified in this matter. It's very noticeable of the demeanor of the officers when they work together vs. working apart, especially pointing out Officer Bailey behavior when Officer Boone isn't around. Officer Boone is considered a bully behind the vest due to his street actions. That's my opinion with the facts given. Once again thank you for your time.

## The Complaint I

Reidsville Police Dept: Officers Bailey & Boone Complaints: While dealing with the incidents of the DG employee, it was brought to my attention that I have a warrant for my arrest-failure to appear. Failure to appear for a traffic violation I never committed in the city of Reidsville, for the RPD to give me a traffic violation citation stating I was driving while licenses were revoked.

Since I can provide legal documents to show and prove my two last traffic violations were conducted and handled by NC State Highway Patrol, and nothing from any city police, now I have questions as to why WASN'T protocol conducted in this manner? Why DIDN'T RPD follow protocol within this traffic stop? Their intentions was thinking my daughter was trafficking drugs, per her previous drug history and previous location at time-they were more interested in searching the vehicle without my consent for drugs and to get in the safe located in the trunk of the car.

The traffic violation was given to who the car was registered to which was me, I was home, her and her friends had my car. Now I can provide all necessary documents (nc dmv driving record) proving the date I DID indeed process a NCDL in question. I was able to renew my license on September 28, 2022. Seven days after this incident described below. NC suspended my license when I got my 2nd ticket on US-Highway 29 for excess speed, I went to court, took care of it in district court with a plea. I was given a fine with ninety days to pay.

I attended court on September 14, 2022, and had until December 15, 2022, to pay this fine. When I received my first traffic violation in March of 2022, which was handled by NC State Highway Patrol, I blacked out while driving my vehicle, causing me to damage a church fencing as I lost control of the car. Per DA in ADM court in Wentworth, NC, I needed documentation from the owners of the church stating they did NOT want to pursue legal actions against me for the damages I had caused to their fence.

I did receive such documents from the church's owners. I provided the DA with this information; the DA dismissed this cause. I was only given a citation because I did indeed damage their property, which the Highway patrolman explained to us as he was giving me the citation, which should be March 14, 2022.

Here's the problem with this situation- It hadn't been long since I had purchased a Benz, RPD targeted my daughter in my vehicle, as she left from one parking lot to another parking lot no more than at least 2 to 3k feet away. Rpd swamped in on her, proceeded to search my vehicle, registered to me, I was NOT aware of this search until a crew member of KFC called one of my children to alert us of the situation.

Now, RPD only wanted to talk to me to obtain permission to open the family safe in the trunk of my car. Then, the RPD said that I needed to show ownership of the car. I asked why my daughter was pulled over. RPD stated that it was due to the front window tint on my car, but I have a medical condition that allows me to have the tint at a certain level. I tried to provide that information, but RPD refused it.

The officers from my understanding had a problem at the RCSO, due to the fact the defendant information he gave them was indeed my name, instead of getting my daughters ID, he wrote a citation in my name for DWLR. This officer had to redo his paperwork at the RCSO because he placed my name as the defendant on the citation instead of my daughters. Now, due to his error and not following procedure, I have to show documents to show my innocence.

My daughter was targeted and being watched because she was a low-lower street drug dealer, she has two previous charges due to the location of where she was leaving from Two Brothers store-known drug area, RPD was sitting across the street and saw her speaking with someone and assumed it was a drug transaction, as she left the parking, RPD officers blocked her in, in the back parking lot of KFC.

During this traffic stop it was discovered she DID indeed process (1) piece of drug, with street value of $20-30. My daughter is the one who does NOT have a license. The officer had to make corrected paperwork while trying to process her at the magistrate office in Wentworth, NC. The magistrate became livid with the officer for NOT having his paperwork together before presenting it to him. Due to their error now I have to clear their wrong doings because they did NOT follow protocol.

### North Carolina Middle District Court

IN THE UNITED STATES DISTRICT COURT FOR THE MIDDLE DISTRICT OF NORTH CAROLINA GREENSBORO DIVISION

ASHLEY DESEIRAY BRITT,

  Plaintiffs,
v.

ROCKINGHAM COUNTY DISTRICT ATTORNEY KATHRYN L. GREGG, in her individual and official capacities; KEVIN KETCHIE, in his individual and official capacities; CHRIS BAILEY, in his individual and official capacities: GREGORY BOONE, in his individual and capacities,

Defendants.

**COMES NOW** Plaintiff Ashley Deseiray Britt states the following as her Complaint against the defendants: Kathryn L. Gregg, Christopher Bailey Gregory Boone, and Kevin Ketchie, individually and in their capacities as North Carolina District Attorney; City of Reidsville, Police Officers; and North Carolina State Bar Officians. Ms. Britt states she was a victim of a pattern or practice of discriminatory law enforcement activities directed against convicted drug dealers in Rockingham County.

## INTRODUCTION

1. This discriminatory conduct deprives the plaintiff of her rights under the Fourth and Fourteenth Amendments of the United States Constitution. Claiming city officials made disparaging remarks about her during this investigation before and after the incident, whose reputation was profoundly damaged, and that the incident violated her rights. Today, the harassment and retaliation continue, causing Ms. Britt immense psychological harm and reputational damage.

2. After filing several complaints with local government agencies regarding law enforcement misconduct, the defendants displayed and

performed retaliation behaviors while prosecuting Ms. Britt's case—State of North Carolina vs. Ashley Deseiray Britt, 22CRS74.

3. The City, County, and Individual Defendants have violated Ms. Britt's rights under federal and state law. As a matter of urgency, this complaint seeks damages and declaratory relief to rectify the significant harm they inflicted upon her.

4. In September 2022, Plaintiff Ashley Britt was and still is considered a Caswell County, North Carolina resident. Ms. Britt has made several court appearances regarding the traffic stop from September 20, 2022, beginning in October 2022, until May 14, 2024, and all other times relevant to this claim.

5 Ms. Britt has been on supervised probation starting in May 2022; during a scheduled appointment in July with whom Ms. Britt expected to be held with Stephaine, the then-current probation officer—instead, Ms. Britt visited with Kevin Ketchie, another probation officer in Rockingham County, North Carolina.

6. After Ms. Britt's first visit with Mr. Ketchie, before the visit, Ms. Britt was not aware that she would no longer be reporting to Stephaine Doe. Mr.

Ketchie was her new officer. Ms. Britt was unaware of the change in her probation officer. Ms. Britt requested out-of-county probation. Ms. Britt's request was approved in July 2022.

7. From July 2022 until the present, Ms. Britt has been under the supervision of Caswell County Probation Officer William Brewer. Over the past two years, Ms. Britt claims she's a victim of patterned "or" practiced behavior by law enforcement.

8. Judge McGhee revoked Ms. Britt's probation on August 29, 2022, sentencing Ms. Britt to 13-27 months in the North Carolina Department of Adult Corrections. On October 6, 2023, at 10:45 am, the late Judge Stanley Allen released Ms. Britt from NCDAC with a signed Consent Order with specific terms and conditions outlined by himself.

9. From October 6, 2023, until May 14, 2024, Ms. Britt has been refused twice, asking the Courts to be placed on unsupervised probation for the remainder of her probation term despite discussing the matter with her current probation officer.

10. On May 14, 2024, Mr. Brewer was willing to submit his recommendations to the Courts, but

Judge Berlin denied doing so after listening to defendant Gregg's statement.

## **JURISDICTION AND VENUE**

11. This Court has jurisdiction to hear the Plaintiff's claims according to 28 U.S.C.§§ 1331, 1343, and 1367.

12. This action is brought according to 42 U.S.C. § 1983 for acts committed by the defendants under color of law that deprived the plaintiff of her rights under the First, Fourth, and Fourteenth Amendments of the United States Constitution.

13. This court has original jurisdiction over the plaintiffs' federal claim under 28 U.S.C. §§ 1331 and 28 U.S.C. § 1343(a)(3).

14. This case arises under the common law and the Constitution of the State of North Carolina. This Court has pendent jurisdiction over plaintiffs' state law claims under 28 U.S.C. §§ 1367.

15. This Court also has jurisdiction under the Declaratory Judgment Act, 28 U.S.C. §§ 2201–02.12.

16. Almost all material events giving rise to this cause of action occurred in Caswell and

Rockingham Counties, North Carolina. Based on information and belief, defendants Kathryn Gregg, Chris Bailey, Gregory Boone, Kevin Ketchie, and Scott Skidmore reside in Rockingham County.

17. Almost all material events giving rise to this case of action occurred in Caswell and Rockingham Counties, North Carolina. Based on information and belief, defendant Jason Keith resides in Guilford County. Under 28 U.S.C. §§ 1391(b), the venue is proper in the United States District Court for the Middle District of North Carolina.

18. The venue is proper in the U.S. District Court for the Middle District of North Carolina under 28 U.S.C. § 1391(b)(2) because a substantial part of the acts that gave rise to this lawsuit occurred in this judicial district. This district is also an appropriate venue under 28 U.S.C. § 1391(b)(1) because Defendants reside in this judicial district.

## **PARTIES**

19. Plaintiff Ashley Deseiray Britt is a citizen and resident of Caswell County, North Carolina.

20. Defendant City of Reidsville (after this "City") is a municipal corporation located in

Rockingham County and organized under the laws of the State of North Carolina.

21. The City of Reidsville, as the Defendant, bears the utmost responsibility for the policies, practices, and customs of its Police Department, which are currently under scrutiny in this complaint. This legal document underlines the weight of their actions.

22. Defendant Gregory Boone, an officer with the Reidsville Police Department, is being sued in his capacity. It is crucial to note that at all times relevant to the material incidents in this complaint, he acted within the scope of his employment and under the color of law, thereby amplifying the gravity of the situation.

23. Defendant Chris Bailey, an officer with the Reidsville Police Department, is being sued in his capacity. It is crucial to note that he acted within the scope of his employment and under the color of law at all relevant times relevant to the material incidents in this complaint, thereby amplifying the gravity of the situation.

24. Defendant Kevin Ketchie, an employee of the North Carolina Judicial System, is being sued in her individual and official capacities. It is crucial to

note that at all times relevant to the material incidents in this complaint, he acted within the scope of her employment and under the color of law, thereby amplifying the gravity of the situation.

25. Defendant Kathryn L. Gregg was appointed District Attorney in Prosecutorial District 22, serving Rockingham and Caswell counties, on March 28, 2024. The primary duty of the District Attorney is to prosecute all criminal cases filed in the district.

26. The District Attorney represents the state in all criminal and juvenile matters. In addition, the District Attorney is responsible for preparing the criminal trial docket and advising law enforcement officers in the district. In this office.

27. Defendant Kathryn L. Gregg is to represent the State with integrity and professionalism while protecting victims and their rights in pursuing justice. At all times pertinent to the material incidents in this complaint, she acted within the scope of her employment and under color of law, further emphasizing the seriousness of the situation.

## BACKGROUND

28. The complaint alleged that during the conference on June 2, 2023, the plaintiff engaged in a conversation with then-attorney Jason Keith about the plaintiff's court hearing scheduled for Monday, June 5, 2023. The conference was held at NxtGenLaw, Jason Keith's law office, 100 S. Elm Street, Suite 100, Greensboro, NC 27401.

29. Keith was retained to represent the plaintiff in Rockingham County Superior Court matters. Rockingham County Superior Court Case File No. 22CRS 74 and 22CRS 75.

30. On June 2, 2023, Keith met with Ashley Britt, the plaintiff, her mother, and her grandmother. When Keith walked in at the beginning of the conference, he mentioned the plaintiff's attire and the persons she was in attendance with during the meeting. "Keith talked about his client's attire: " Oh, I see you got the chains on."

31. He also referred to the persons in attendance with the plaintiff during the conference: "You got the whole family in here." At the beginning of the meeting, Keith told the plaintiff's mother, Latoye Britt, "I don't know whether you know this or not, but Katy Gregg has it out for your daughter."

32. During the conference, the plaintiff believed Keith openly revealed why the defendant held a

vendetta; Keith stated, "The defendant wanted the plaintiff to go to prison because she kept getting new charges while being on probation." and described the method in detail via text message what the defendants' method was going to be to secure sentencing and send the plaintiff to prison.

33. "It doesn't matter whether she's guilty of the new charges. I will put the officer on the stand to have the judge convict her for probation violation."

34. During the conference, Keith commented on the defendant's prosecution over the plaintiff's matter. Keith stated, "One of the main reasons why Ross didn't take your case is because Katy got a big stance in your case."

35. "You don't have a working relationship, and you're not one of those people we got working behind the scenes." Keith texted the defendant during the conference. Communicating with the defendant via text message referencing the upcoming court date of June 5, 2023, Keith, with phone in hand, read aloud the defendant's response to his client:

36. "Mr. Keith, I know you're going to contest these drug charges, but let me tell you what I am going to do; I'm going to put the officer on the

stand; I'm going to have the officer testify that she was driving without a license, and on that fact alone, I will have her probation revoked."

37. The Plaintiff filed a complaint with the North Carolina State Bar against J. Keith on or about June 28, 2023, NC Bar Case File No. 23G0943. The Plaintiff filed a complaint with the North Carolina State Bar against K. Gregg on or about August 09, 2023, NC Bar Case File No. 23G0944.

38. Both NC Bar Grievance Case File Nos. 23G0943 and 23G0944 were reviewed by a member of the North Carolina State Bar Association (in the future, the "NCSB"); the NCSB, in its January 2024 response, states that there were no substantial findings to the complaint in the NCSB Case File No. 23G0944, and therefore, the grievance was closed.

39. On May 25, 2022, the plaintiff was placed on supervised probation with a suspended sentence of thirteen (13) to twenty-five (25) months under the supervision of P.O. Stephaine Doe.

40. Probation Officer Stephaine will use Doe's last name until the exact last name is revealed. From May 2022 until June 2022, the plaintiff reported to

Stephaine Doe of the Rockingham County Parole and Probation office.

41. The plaintiff states that the officers were changed in late June or early July without providing notice of the officer change or any communication regarding the officers and the plaintiffs.

42. The plaintiff arrived at the scheduled appointment time arranged with Stephanie Doe. Once there, however, the plaintiff did not meet with Stephanie Doe; instead, the plaintiff met with Kevin Ketchie.

43. The plaintiff states that during this first visit, Mr. Ketchie was rude, discourteous, and impolite, and Mr. Kethcie was perceived to have an attitude toward Ms. Britt. However, again, this was her very first encounter.

44. After the first visit, the plaintiff requested to be transferred to out-of-county probation, and at least three incidents occurred via text messages between Officer Ketchie and Ms. Britt.

45. Mr. Ketchie was again rude and discourteous toward Ms. Britt, ex. "When I say to be home, I mean to stay until I get there, no matter how long I take." "Do you want to be locked up for

the weekend? Cause I have no problem locking you up."

46. The plaintiff states that Mr. Ketchie's behavior toward her was one of several reasons she requested out-of-county probation.

47. After hearing confirmation from then-retained counsel Jason Keith in June 2022, the plaintiff stated that the intentions were discussed verbally in detail regarding how defendant Gregg would convict Ms. Britt of driving while her license was revoked.

48. The plaintiff states that Jason Keith verbally communicated a text from defendant Gregg regarding Ms. Britt and her case matter, scheduled on June 5, 2023.

49. His high and visibly strong intentions toward Ms. Britt were indicated to support the personal feelings and vindictive behavior displayed by Defendant Gregg when he read the text message aloud.

50. Upon release on October 6, 2023, the plaintiff reported to William Brewer, North Carolina Adult and Probation Officer in Caswell County. Upon release on October 6, 2023, the plaintiff

reported to William Brewer, North Carolina Adult and Probation Officer in Caswell County.

51. The plaintiff states that for the remainder of the supervised probation terms before and after the court trial date, August 29, 2023, Consent Order signed by the late Judge S. Allen, the plaintiff was confined to a home monitoring device for six months after the court trial date, October 6, 2023.

52. Upon being released on October 6, 2023, the plaintiff was placed on an electronic monitoring device for six (6) months under the supervision of William Brewer. After six (6) months of electronic monitoring, Mr. Brewer removed the electronic monitoring device.

53. The consent order needs to state the specific details necessary for the terms and conditions of the consent order, signed by the late S. Allen on October 6, 2023.

54. Upon being released on October 6, 2023, the plaintiff appeared in court a day a month for the past six (6) months regarding the disposition of case file number 22 CRS 74.

55. Upon being released on October 6, 2023, the plaintiff twice requested to be transferred to

unsupervised probation due to completing all the terms and conditions and being on probation for the half-of-sentence requirement required to request such privilege.

56. The plaintiff states that before entering a request for unsupervised probation, the plaintiff spoke with Mr. Brewer. Mr. Brewer, in return, contacted the plaintiff's attorney, asking if there were any objections to the plaintiff being transferred to unsupervised probation.

57. After several days, the plaintiff's attorney emailed Mr. Brewer, apologizing for his delay. He also stated that he did not object to the plaintiff's motions for unsupervised probation.

58. The plaintiff states that after this conversation, the court clerk in Caswell County ignored the first request for unsupervised probation. As the plaintiff states, she has yet to receive a court date.

59. The plaintiff states that another request was submitted to the court clerk in Caswell County before this motion was submitted, with the approval of probation officer William Brewer.

60. The plaintiff's second motion was granted a court trial date of May 14, 2024.

## FIRST CAUSE OF ACTION

Plaintiff restates and realizes all preceding paragraphs as if fully set forth herein.

61. The allegations in the preceding paragraphs are incorporated by reference, as stated in Paragraphs 1-60.

62. The plaintiff states that, based on all the behaviors displayed by Gregg, Ketchie, Bailey, Boone, Keith, and Skidmore before August 29, 2023, she believes she's a victim of a Pattern or Practice of law enforcement.

63. The plaintiff's statement on August 29, 2023, was truthful and was compelled by the defendant's actions. "willful misconduct in office" has been defined in other proceedings involving judges. In that context, the term is "the improper or wrongful use of the power of her office by a judge acting intentionally, or with gross unconcern for her conduct, and generally in bad faith." In re Nowell, 293 N. C. 235, 248, 237 S. E. 2d 246 (1977).

64. The plaintiff's statement was constitutionally protected in that she exercised her constitutional right to free speech, guaranteed by the First Amendment to the United States Constitution.

65. The plaintiff's rights and obligations warranted by her statement were truthful during and after the August 29, 2023, court appearance. They outweighed any claimed interest by defendant Gregg or the Rockingham County District Attorney's office.

66. Defendant Gregg displayed retaliation and premeditation methods for the termination of Britt's probation term. There was no legitimate, nondiscriminatory reason to terminate Britt's probation before the August 29, 2023 conviction. By revoking Britt's probation term in retaliation for her official complaint against Reidsville Police Officers Chris Bailey and Greg Boone, defendant Gregg violated Britt's rights under the United States Constitution's First Amendment, violating 42 U.S.C. § 1983.

67. The defendant's actions were done maliciously, willfully, wantonly, or in a manner that demonstrates reckless disregard for Britt's rights. As a result of the defendant's conduct, Britt is entitled to recover punitive damages. As a

proximate result of the defendant's wrongful conduct, Britt has suffered emotional distress, humiliation, loss of reputation, and other damages.

68. The defendant's actions were done maliciously, willfully, wantonly, or in a manner that demonstrates reckless disregard for Britt's rights. During the court appearance on August 29, 2023, defendant Gregg knew the statements made by herself, Bailey, Boone, and Ketchie were false statements given to the courts, making the defendants violate the Rules of Professional Conduct.

69. The defendant's actions were done maliciously, willfully, wantonly, or in a manner that demonstrates reckless disregard for Britt's rights. During her court appearance on May 14, 2024, defendant Gregg knew the statements she made to Judge Berlin during the court appearance on May 14, 2024, were false statements given to the courts, making the defendants violate the Rules of Professional Conduct.

70. The defendant's actions were malicious, willful, wantonly, or in a manner that demonstrates reckless disregard for Britt's rights.

71. Rule 3.3(a)(1) of the Revised Rules of Professional Conduct provides that a lawyer shall not knowingly make a false statement of a material fact or law to a tribunal."

72. Defendant Gregg violated Rule 3.3(a)(1) by knowingly making a false statement of material fact to Judge McGee during a court appearance on August 29, 2023, in Rockingham County Superior Court.

73. Defendant Gregg violated Rule 3.3(a)(1) by knowingly making a false statement of material fact to Judge Berlin during a court appearance on May 14, 2024, in Caswell County Superior Court.

74. The defendant's actions were malicious, willful, wantonly, or in a manner that demonstrates reckless disregard for Britt's rights.

75. Rule 8.4(a) of the Revised Rules of Professional Conduct provides that "(i)t is professional misconduct for a lawyer to violate or attempt to violate the Rules of Professional Conduct."

76. Rule 8.4(c) of the Revised Rules of Professional Conduct provides that "(i)t is professional misconduct for a lawyer to… engage in conduct involving dishonesty, fraud, deceit or

misrepresentation that reflects adversely on the lawyer's fitness as a lawyer."

## THE SECOND CAUSE OF ACTION

77. All facts in this complaint were committed against the plaintiff and, in the plaintiff's view, are to be found by clear, compelling, and convincing evidence.

78. All the alleged violations arose from the plaintiff's initial connection with then-retained Jason Keith and then-Rockingham County Assistant District Attorney.

79. The plaintiff was initially charged with possession of crack cocaine and driving while license was revoked. Later was indicted for Possession with intent to sell and deliver in November 2022.

80. The Plaintiff was initially indicted for felony possession of cocaine with intent to sell and deliver, which constituted the plaintiff being charged with a probation violation for a traffic stop conducted on September 20, 2022, by Reidsville Police Department Officers Chris Bailey and Gregory Boone.

81. The plaintiff states that Officer Bailey was seen patrolling the area as the plaintiff was in the store speaking with a relative; the plaintiff states Officer Bailey displayed pattern "or " practice behaviors toward the plaintiff before initially proceeding to conduct the traffic stop.

82. The plaintiff states that Officer Bailey noted that he made the traffic stop because the vehicle violated the tint rules and guidelines according to the state of North Carolina. Although Officer Bailey stated this was the reason for the nature of the stop, the plaintiff was not issued a citation for violating the tint during the stop.

83. The plaintiff states that during the traffic stop on September 20, 2022, Officer Bailey requested backup assistance because he did not have a tint reader at the stop.

84. The plaintiff stated that in September 2023, she was transported to the North Carolina Department of Adult Correction from the Rockingham County Detention Center while in NCDAC custody.

85. The Reidsville Internal Affairs Division of the Reidsville Police Department sent certified letters to the plaintiff and the plaintiff's mother

regarding the complaint against Officers Bailey and Boone.

86. The plaintiff states that Internal Affairs found Officer Bailey and Boone to have committed misconduct during the September 20, 2022 traffic stop. Rockingham County did not acknowledge the misconduct of its law enforcement officers and justice center.

87. The plaintiff tends to show that RPD officers "intentionally and recklessly" provided false and misleading information to a magistrate to secure his arrest on September 20, 2022. That's because she was arrested after police officers illegally searched the vehicle in her possession at the time of the traffic stop.

88. The plaintiff states the search was based on the officer's conversation while en route to the scene; conversation could be heard regarding the plaintiff's past drug conviction, saying, "She's a convicted drug dealer." and whether or not the plaintiff attended school with one of the officers.

89. Once arriving at the scene, Officer Boone commented regarding the plaintiff's hair: " That was not her hair, that it was weed." He stated he

didn't believe the hair belonged to the plaintiff and that it was weed.

90. The plaintiff states that starting in June 2023, she wrote grievances against RPD officers Chris Bailey and Gregory Boone, who filed with RPD. On September 13, 2023, the RPD Internal Affairs Division found Officers Bailey and Boone had conducted misconduct during its September 20, 2022, traffic stop.

91. The plaintiff states that starting in June 2023, she wrote grievances against Rockingham County Assistant District Attorney Kathryn L. Gregg and Attorney Jason Keith for unethical practices she felt were being committed against her.

92. The plaintiff presents questions for review broadly concerning the issues of:

> (1) whether the indictment should have been quashed and the charges dismissed because the prosecution against him was based on institutional selective prosecution;

> (2) whether the superseding indictment should have been quashed and the charges dismissed because of unconstitutional vindictive prosecution;

(3) the sufficiency of the evidence to withstand plaintiff's motion to dismiss; and

(4) whether the court abused its discretion in imposing a prison term of 13-27 months in the custody of the North Carolina

Department of Adult Corrections for probation violation Case File No. 22CRS74. <u>Law Officials-</u>

Reidsville Police Department Chris Bailey and Gregory Boone; ADA—Rockingham County Kathryn Gregg; Probation Officer Kevin Ketchie; District Attorney Kathryn Gregg; and Jason Keith.

## **THIRD CAUSE FOR ACTION**

93. The plaintiff alleges that on critical dates, such as August 29, 2023, the police and Rockingham County District Attorney's Office, Kathryn L. Gregg, provided false and misleading information to Superior Court Judge McGee regarding case matter 22CRS74.

94. The RPD officer stated that the probable cause for the stop was the vehicle's violation of the North Carolina General Statute for tinting.

95. The plaintiff states these alleged actions led to the plaintiff's conviction for probation violation and subsequent sentencing to 13-25 months in the

North Carolina Department of Adult Corrections on August 29, 2023.

96. Assistant District Attorney Kathryn Gregg displayed premeditated behaviors when Jason Keith expressed those behaviors aloud via a text message sent by Gregg during the plaintiff's meeting on June 2, 2023, at Jason Keith's law office.

97. The plaintiff states that on August 29, 2023, those premeditated behaviors described by Jason Keith on June 2, 2023, that of Kathryn Gregg, were utilized to benefit the defendants when RPD Officer Bailey was not truthful with his court testimony.

98. The plaintiff states that before the court trial on August 29, 2023, Assistant District Attorney Kathryn Gregg described the plan to convict the plaintiff of a probation violation for driving while her license was revoked from a traffic stop on September 20, 2022.

99. Before the trial, the plaintiff and family members read the lips of Rockingham County District Attorney Kathryn L. Gregg, who initially asked the RPD officer to commit perjury by saying, "On September 20, 2022, he saw Ashley Britt get in and out of the car." "She was driving without a license."

100. The RPD officer testified to seeing the plaintiff get in and out of the car when the RPD officer did not know the plaintiff was driving the vehicle.

101. The plaintiff states that on August 29, 2023, those premeditated behaviors described by Jason Keith on June 2, 2023, that of Kathryn Gregg, were utilized to benefit the defendants when RPD Officer Bailey was not truthful with his court testimony.

102. Complaints had been filed against Officers Bailey and Boone during the traffic stop on September 20, 2022; Officer Bailey presented arresting documents to the magistrate with the citations written in the wrong detainee's name.

103. The plaintiff states that after an investigation by the Reidsville Police Department's Internal Affairs Division. The investigation indicated that after its careful and thorough investigation, Officers Bailey and Boone were found to have committed misconduct during the September 20, 2022 traffic stop.

104. The plaintiff stated that the mother was visibly upset immediately upon sentencing. Before the court trial on August 29, 2023, the plaintiff's

mother had previously filed complaints regarding the unethical practices committed during a traffic stop on September 20, 2022.

105. Furthermore, after sentencing, the plaintiff was placed in the custody of the ("NCDAC").

## FOURTH CAUSE OF ACTION

106. All facts in this complaint were committed against the plaintiff and, in the plaintiff's view, are to be found by clear, compelling, and convincing evidence.

107. The plaintiff states that the defendant has displayed premeditation, dishonesty, perjury behavior, accessory to commit perjury, discrimination, and premeditation and retaliation.

108. The plaintiff states that at all times relevant to being placed on probation, the defendant violated her Civil Rights and First, Fourth, and Fourteenth Amendment Rights; the plaintiff states she was and still is a victim of a victim of the defendant's "Pattern or Practice."

109. The plaintiff states that all relevant times relevant to being placed on probation are under the supervision of William Brewer. Officer Brewer has made several home visits to the defendants'

addresses listed on file, where she states she lived at 691 Mineral Springs Road in Pelham, North Carolina, before being convicted and released on October 6, 2023, and has lived there ever since.

110. The plaintiff states that all times relevant to being placed on probation are under the supervision of William Brewer; she's been a victim of the court's retaliation and premeditation by law enforcement officers and the justice center of Rockingham County, North Carolina.

111. The plaintiff has kept a clean probation history with Officer Brewer. The plaintiff has yet to schedule an appointment with Ketchie before September 20, 2022 and did not fail any drug screens while being placed on probation.

112. The plaintiff filed a complaint against defendant Gregg at the NC State Bar in June 2023; in response to the plaintiff's complaints, the NC State Bar stated that they saw no wrongdoings by either attorney.

113. The plaintiff paid all North Carolina fines and restoration fees, all Rockingham County Clerk of Superior Court Division court costs, and all other penalties imposed by the presiding judge.

114. The plaintiff states there was no legitimate, nondiscriminatory reason to terminate Britt's probation during the August 29, 2023, court appearance, and Gregg displayed retaliation and premeditation methods to terminate Britt's probation term.

115. The plaintiff tends to show before the trial on August 29, 2023, the defendants "intentionally and recklessly" provided false and misleading information to law officials, which led to a conviction for probation violation and subsequent sentencing to 13-27 months in the North Carolina Department of Adult Corrections on August 29, 2023.

116. The plaintiff tends to show during the trial on August 29, 2023, the defendants "intentionally and recklessly" provided false and misleading information to law officials, which led to a conviction for probation violation and subsequent sentencing to 13-27 months in the North Carolina Department of Adult Corrections on August 29, 2023.

117. The plaintiff tends to show that RPD officers "intentionally and recklessly" provided false and misleading information to a magistrate to secure his arrest on September 20, 2022. That's because she was arrested after police officers illegally searched

the vehicle in her possession at the time of the traffic stop.

118. The plaintiff states the search was based on the officer's conversation while en route to the scene; conversation could be heard regarding the plaintiff's past drug conviction, saying, "She's a convicted drug dealer." and whether or not the plaintiff attended school with one of the officers.

## FIFTH CAUSE OF ACTION

119. During the trial on May 14, 2024, the plaintiff tends to show that Defendant Gregg "intentionally and recklessly" provided false and misleading information to Judge Berlin, which led to a denial of the plaintiff's motion to be placed on unsupervised probation for the remainder of the probation term.

120. The plaintiff stated that on August 29, 2023, the plaintiff was found guilty of probation violation and subsequently sentenced to 13-27 months after the plaintiff's observation during the court trial.

121. The plaintiff requested to speak with the lead detective working on an ongoing murder case in Rockingham County. This request was made at the plaintiff's free will.

122. The plaintiff states while being placed in custody on August 29, 2023, the plaintiff requested to speak to the lead detective of an ongoing murder investigation.

123. In the plaintiff's statement to RPD, as being the only eye witness willing to come forward with details of the murder.

124. After speaking with P. Lingle while in custody at Rockingham Detention Center, P. Lingle credited her statement and provided his facts to the Rockingham County District Attorney's Office.

125. The plaintiff states while being placed in custody on August 29, 2023, the plaintiff was taken to jail, strip-searched, and put in a holding cell.

126. The plaintiff's fellow inmates, who likely were already aware of her charges, persistently harassed her and worried for her safety.

127. The plaintiff states that she had already been in fear for her life due to what she'd witnessed months earlier.

128. On several occasions, the plaintiff spent the night at the homes of close family members, such as

her uncle and grandmother, who live outside the city limits.

129. The plaintiff stated while being in the custody of NCDAC and housed at the Rockingham County Detention Center, she was in fear for her life, according to the plaintiff due to housed inmate April Turner communicating directly with the suspected killer.

130. The plaintiff states while being housed at the Rockingham County Detention Center, the plaintiff and her mother received a threat of communication from, according to the plaintiff, through the passage of a housed inmate, April Turner, who was communicating directly with the suspected killer.

131. The plaintiff states while being housed at the Rockingham County Detention Center, the plaintiff and her mother received a threat of communication from, according to the plaintiff, through the passage of a housed inmate, April Turner, who communicated the threat to the plaintiff, via hollering from jail cell to jail cell, "Yo Britt, Yg said to keep her fucking name out of your mouth."

132. Later on that day, the same inmate delivered another message stating that the message wasn't for you; it was for your mama. In response to the

threat, the plaintiff said, "Ok, bet let me call home and tell my mama."

133. This was the second threatening message received by the murder suspect. The plaintiff said that before being detained on August 29, 2023.

134. The plaintiff states the murder suspect had previously threatened her by telling the plaintiff's sibling, "Yo tell yo sister, Ashley Britt, she can get it too. I'll lay her down, too. When I see her, it's on sight." After the plaintiff learned of this message, the plaintiff began leaving the city earlier than usual.

135. The plaintiff states that from August 29, 2023, until October 6, 2023, she was in the custody of the as of October 6, 2023, for 38 days. While in custody, the plaintiff's counsel ended communication with the plaintiff's mother.

136. The plaintiff states that counsel had previously spoken with her mother; family members repeatedly tried to contact the plaintiff's counsel via emails, telephone office, and courthouse visits; the plaintiff's family provided counsel with documents proving the plaintiff's allegations were true via electronic and a paper copy; and the completion of an investigation conducted by the Internal Affairs of

the Reidsville Police Department on September 13, 2023.

137. The plaintiff also states Skidmore knew of the vendetta displayed by Defendant Gregg toward the plaintiff before August 29, 2023.

138. The plaintiff states that neither attorney had made a motion to remove Defendant Gregg from the plaintiff case matter despite having filed a complaint with the North Carolina State Bar.

139. Scott Skidmore—The plaintiff states that when she became in NCDAC's custody, counsel didn't represent her to the best of his ability. One reason was that when the plaintiff asked counsel on several different occasions if "he'd looked at the emails, had he been listening to his voicemails, and on each occasion, these questions were asked, and the response was one of the three following comments.

(1) "No, I haven't; I've been too busy."

(2) "I haven't had time." (3) "Call and set up an appointment with my office, and we'll talk about it." These activities began in June 2023.

140. Within the first 15 days of incarceration, the plaintiff stated that counsel lacked communication with family members; the counsel told the plaintiff's family, "He had to get a judge to overturn her conviction and needed to be signed by a judge."

141. The plaintiff states that counsel displayed upset when making the following comment regarding the plaintiff requesting to speak with the lead detective of an ongoing murder investigation. "I guess she just cut me out of the deal, didn't she?"

142. The plaintiff states that it's her opinion that counsel only gathered certain information but did not intend to use it to benefit the plaintiff. For example, the plaintiff told counsel of an audio recording of a confession.

143. Ms. Britt, the mother, was to retrieve the recording and take it to counsel. Ms. Britt and her son met at Scott Skidmore's law office, where she let Skidmore listen to the recording.

144. Skidmore told Ms. Britt what she had provided wasn't enough to help him; it would do anything." He then stated, "Well, the good thing is that the detective on the case believes her." At this moment, Ms. Britt questioned the overturned conviction.

145. The plaintiff stated that counsel said, "He'd have to get a judge to sign a new judgment. He could ask Allen and should not have a problem with it.

146. Within 38 days, the plaintiff was transferred to the NC Department of Corrections for Women; when family members contacted the plaintiff's counsel, he stated, "I had no idea she was gone; I'll get her back as soon as possible."

147. The plaintiff also states counsel told the plaintiff's mother, "You writing all these letters and talking junk about the cops isn't helping your daughter's case. I can't get her a better deal because of all your letters."

148. The plaintiff states that beginning in June 2023, she began to complain about the misconduct being committed against her with two counsels aware of the plaintiff's allegations, as neither counsel believed the plaintiff nor took the plaintiff seriously with the allegations.

149. The plaintiff's mother started researching this case matter once misconduct was witnessed during several court appearances. Jason Keith told

the plaintiff's mother, "You know Katy Gregg has it out for your daughter, right?"

150. The behaviors described by then-retained counsel Jason Keith on June 2, 2022, as well as the intentions and methods premeditated that would be utilized to secure the plaintiff's conviction for probation violation and driving while her license was revoked.

## **SIXTH CAUSE OF ACTION**

151. The plaintiff claimed the defendants "intentionally and recklessly" provided false and misleading information to law officials, leading to the plaintiff's continuous court appearances after October 6, 2023.

152. The plaintiff asserts that Defendant Gregg was absent at the "special Session on October 6, 2023, Rockingham County, Superior Court Division. The attendees were Attorney Scott Skidmore, District Attorney Jason Ramey, and Chief Assistant District Attorney Veronica Schooley.

153. The plaintiff's counsel presented the courts with its prepared Motion For Appropriate Relief,

which was rejected during a "special Session" on October 6, 2023, by presiding late judge Stanley Allen.

154. The plaintiff refused to sign the Motion For Appropriate Relief, which will only reflect the signature of the plaintiff's counsel, Scott Skidmore.

155. The plaintiff alleges that on critical dates, such as May 14, 2024, Rockingham County District Attorney Kathryn L. Gregg provided false and misleading information to Superior Court Judge Berlin regarding probation case matter 22CRS74.

156. The plaintiff has made seven court appearances in the matter. The seventh is May 14, 2024, in Caswell County Superior Court, with Judge Berlin as the presiding judge.

157. The plaintiff concludes that Defendant Gregg was not truthful in her statement to Judge Berlin on May 14, 2024, regarding the judge's rejection of its Motion For Appropriate Relief for the plaintiff upon release from the North Carolina Department of Adult Correction ("NCDAC") on October 6, 2023.

158. The plaintiff states that the late Judge Stanley Allen, on October 6, 2023, at 10:15 am.,

rejected the state's Motion For Appropriate Relief requesting the order be written over in the plaintiff's case matter.

159. While presiding, Judge Allen outlined the terms and conditions of the Consent Order, ordering each party to prepare a new order for the plaintiff's immediate release, and the plaintiff was not to be transported to the NCDAC for processing but released from the Rockingham County Detention Center.

160. The plaintiff states that the late Judge Stanley Allen had already considered and signed the new Consent Order with terms and conditions "specially outlined" by himself on October 6, 2023, at 10:45 a.m.

161. As part of the Consent Order, the plaintiff was to remain active with the RPD regarding the investigation of the ongoing murder, along with all the other terms and conditions previously set forth.

162. Judge Allen made the following comment before issuing the terms and conditions of the Consent Order: "I can not change or override another Superior judge ruling and sentencing, but I can modify the judgment."

163. The plaintiff states that since filing complaints regarding the unethical practices of Kathryn Gregg, Jason Keith, Christopher Bailey, and Gregory Boone, in this case, she has been harassed, targeted, unlawfully convicted, and detained; after being released,

164. Law officials were still detaining the plaintiff. The plaintiff was instructed to be placed on a home electronic monitoring device set forth by the prosecution. With the monitoring device, the plaintiff's curfew was at 11:00 p.m.

165. The plaintiff wore a monitoring device for six months and 180 days of confinement due to the misconduct of RPD officers and Rockingham County's District Attorney, Kathryn Gregg.

166. The plaintiff states that before the court trial on August 29, 2023, then Assistant District Attorney Kathryn Gregg knew Mr. Brewer became the plaintiff's probation officer once the plaintiff requested to be placed out of the county after an investigation had not been conducted per the report of misconduct committed by the plaintiff's original probation officer, Kevin Ketchie.

167. During the trial, Judge Berlin commented: "I don't have a problem transferring you to unsupervised probation.

168. And I don't want to transfer you, and you're violated within the 12 months of being unsupervised. I need more information, and I need to speak with DA Gregg before I can make a decision."

169. The plaintiff concluded that the defendant was not present during the first part of the trial on May 14, 2024, when Judge Berlin requested the presence of defendant Gregg or to speak with her and to gain more information concerning the case matter. The plaintiff states that after listening to Judge Berlin's decision, the plaintiff received a new trial date, dated late June.

170. The plaintiff left the court session and returned home. After about 30 minutes of being home, someone from the Caswell County clerk of court's office phoned the plaintiff, asking her for her location as she was needed back for trial.

171. The plaintiff said to the person on the phone, "Oh, I thought I was finished; they gave me a court date in June." The person on the phone asked how

long it would take the plaintiff to get there to get back to the courthouse.

172. The plaintiff stayed about 5 to 10 minutes, and she was on the way. The plaintiff and her mother left, arriving at the court at approximately 12:05-12:15 pm.

173. The plaintiff concludes that Defendant Gregg was not truthful in her statement to Judge Berlin on May 14, 2024, regarding the contents of the Consent Order signed by the judge.

174. The plaintiff concludes that the defendant was present during the second part of the trial on May 14, 2024, when Judge Berlin requested her presence.

175. The defendant testified, and Judge Berlin listened to the plaintiff testify. Defendant Gregg did not have a copy of the Motion For Appropriate Relief or the Consent Order regarding the Court's judgment on October 6, 2023.

176. The plaintiff states that after listening, Caswell County's Superior Court Judge Berlin asked the defendant if she had a copy of the Motion. The defendant replied, "No, but I can pull it up on

my phone." Judge Berlin declined to review the defendant's phone to review the documents.

177. The plaintiff states that after listening to the defendant testify, the plaintiff tried to object to the Court's statement regarding the terms and conditions of the plaintiff's signed Motion agreement on October 6, 2023. Accordingly, the plaintiff, Judge Berlin, declined to see the actual documentation provided by the plaintiff.

178. The plaintiff states that the current probation officer, William Brewer, did have the authority per the signed Consent Order on October 6, 2023; other terms and conditions could be set forth and modified by the plaintiff's probation officer.

179. The plaintiff concludes that the court did not allow probation officer William Brewer to provide his recommendation for the plaintiff's request once Defendant Gregg was present at the court trial.

180. The plaintiff states that although the plaintiff's probation officer had the authority to suggest, modify, or terminate the plaintiff's probation term, the judge denied hearing his recommendation.

181. The plaintiff states that her first request for unsupervised probation was transferred to the Rockingham County Superior Court Division without her knowledge after the case was given to the Rockingham County Superior Court Division.

182. The plaintiff was never given a court date in the matter, nor was she given any information about what happened with the 2023 request to be placed on unsupervised probation.

## SEVENTH CAUSE OF ACTION

183. During the court trial on May 14, 2024, District Attorney Kathryn Gregg displayed what the plaintiff felt was retaliation by way of continued confinement with the blocking of the plaintiff's request to be transferred to unsupervised probation with recommendations from the plaintiff's current probation officer, William Brewer, Caswell County.

184. The plaintiff concludes that Caswell County Superior Court Judge Berlin denied the plaintiff's request for unsupervised probation on May 14, 2024, because the defendant provided false and misleading information regarding the terms and conditions of the plaintiff's Motion For Appropriate Relief.

185. The plaintiff states that the current probation officer, William Brewer, called the plaintiff into a scheduled meeting early to remove the monitor, saying, "The judge did not give any specific terms and conditions regarding the monitoring device." nor does it state any specific details regarding the plaintiff's reason or time-limited of wearing the device.

186. The plaintiff states that at the May 14, 2024, court trial and at the time of this filing, the plaintiff was no longer required to wear the electronic monitoring device. Neither defendant noticed the defendant was no longer wearing the home electronic monitoring device.

187. The plaintiff states that the device had been removed for at least 30 to 45 days, and the plaintiff states that neither defendant knew of the device being removed from the plaintiff.

188. The plaintiff states that before the May 14, 2024, trial hearing, she'd previously spoken with probation officer William Brewer twice regarding the plaintiff's transfer to unsupervised probation for a reminder of the plaintiff's probation term.

189. The plaintiff states that Mr. Brewer noted that he would need to speak with the plaintiff's

counsel to see if he has any objections to the plaintiff being transferred to unsupervised probation.

190. The plaintiff's counsel replied to Mr. Brewer via email, stating, "Sorry for the delayed reply; no, I don't have any objections to her being placed on unsupervised probation.

191. The plaintiff states her second request for unsupervised probation was at the recommendation of probation officer William Brewer in 2024. The plaintiff states, "Mr. Brewer has expressed several times during the scheduled appointments and home visits the plaintiff's probation term was a waste of his time, as there was not anything to supervise the plaintiff on."

192. The plaintiff concludes that Defendant Gregg was not truthful in her statement to Judge Berlin on May 14, 2024, regarding the plaintiff's request to be transferred to unsupervised probation.

193. Defendant Gregg told Judge Berlin that "the plaintiff got herself out of a sentence by waiting to come forward about a murder after she was convicted."

194. Defendant Gregg told Judge Berlin, "If the plaintiff wanted to work out of the county, then she needs to move out." Defendant Gregg also told Judge Berlin, "The plaintiff skipped out on a prison sentence."

195. This plaintiff states that the denial was greatly weighed on the statement of the plaintiff's request for unsupervised probation on May 14, 2024, due to the defendant providing false and misleading information regarding the actual terms and conditions of the Consent Order.

196. The plaintiff believes she's a victim of malicious prosecution. The prosecutor was heavily involved with the plaintiff's original case, filing 22CRS74.

197. The plaintiff states Keith knew of Defendant Gregg's feelings toward their client, especially what Keith said to the plaintiff's mother on June 2, 2023, during a meeting at the law office of Jason Keith, S. Elm Street, Greensboro, NC. "I don't know whether you know this, but Katy Gregg has it out for your daughter."

198. The plaintiff states that if Keith knew of Defendant Gregg's intentions before the plaintiff's appearance in court.

199. The plaintiff states both Keith and Skidmore knew the vendetta displayed by defendant Gregg toward the plaintiff before August 29, 2023.

200. The plaintiff states that counsel had communicated effectively and reviewed the information provided by providing actual proof for alleged allegations of misconduct by law enforcement.

201. The plaintiff would have proven her case and shown the misconduct committed against the plaintiff. If the attorneys had asked to remove defendant Gregg due to displayed and expressed vendetta held for the plaintiff, the plaintiff's probation would most likely not have been violated.

202. The plaintiff states that if Keith and Skidmore had asked to remove defendant Gregg due to displayed and expressed vendetta held for the plaintiff, the plaintiff's probation would most likely not have been violated.

203. The plaintiff states that if both retained counsels had communicated effectively and reviewed the information provided, with providing actual proof for alleged allegations of misconduct by law enforcement, the plaintiff would have

proven her case and shown the misconduct being committed against her.

204. The plaintiff states that she has had ineffective counsel during the probation violation matter and doesn't believe counsel represented her to the best of their abilities.

## EIGHTH CAUSE OF ACTION

205. The plaintiff's rights and obligations warranted by her statement were truthful during and after the August 29, 2023, court appearance.

206. They outweighed any claimed interest by defendant Gregg or the Rockingham County District Attorney's office.

207. The plaintiff states that between August 29, 2023, and October 6, 2023, she was falsely convicted and imprisoned in Superior Court, Rockingham County.

208. The plaintiff stated that on August 29, 2023, she witnessed defendant Gregg ask Bailey to commit perjury during his testimony in open court regarding the probation of Ashley Britt.

209. The plaintiff states that on August 29, 2023, she witnessed Christopher Bailey commit perjury during his testimony in open court regarding the probation of Ashley Britt.

210. The plaintiff states that on August 29, 2023, defendant Gregg did not notify the courts of an open or refusal of a plea in May 2023, complaints filed against other defendants named above, with the North Carolina State Bar Associate and Reidsville Police Department, and conflict of interest.

211. The plaintiff states that on August 29, 2023, the defendant's statement to the courts was falsely made to purposely convict the plaintiff of driving on a revoked license, a probation violation.

212. The plaintiff states that after hearing the state evidence, her probation was revoked due to the untruthful testimony of law enforcement and Gregg's involvement with accessory to commit perjury.

213. The plaintiff states that on August 29, 2023, defendant Gregg did not notify the courts of an open complaint pending at the time of sentencing.

214. On their face, and as applied to Ms. Britt's conviction and all related court trial matters, it is an unconstitutional infringement of freedom of speech under the federal and state constitutions.

215. The plaintiff's statement on August 29, 2023, was truthful and was compelled by the defendant's actions. According to 42 U.S.C. § 1983, this claim is brought against defendants Gregg, Ketchie, Keith, Bailey, Skidmore, and Boone in their official and individual capacities.

216. The plaintiff states that a plea offer for sentencing concurrently with a guilty conviction for a traffic stop on September 20, 2022, was rejected.

217. The plaintiff filed several complaints regarding the traffic stop on September 20, 2022. The plaintiff had not been convicted or found guilty of the pending September 20, 2022, charges.

218. The advising and coaching of Officer Bailey's submission to commit perjury during his testimony on August 29, 2023.

219. The defendant violated Rule 3.3(a)(1) by failing to correct his false statement of material fact to Judge Mcgee. The defendant knowingly made

false statements during the August 29, 2023, court trial.

220. The plaintiff states her term of probation was revoked because of the false statements made in open court on August 29, 2023. The North Carolina Constitution protected the plaintiff's freedom. There was no legitimate non-discriminatory reason to violate the plaintiff's probation.

221. By terminating the plaintiff's probation in retaliation for her filing complaints with the following agencies, North Carolina State Bar Association and the Reidsville Police Department, the defendant violated the plaintiff's North Carolina Constitution Right.

222. The defendant's actions were done maliciously, willfully, wantonly, or in a manner that demonstrates reckless disregard for Britt's rights. As a result of the defendant's conduct, Britt is entitled to recover punitive damages. As a proximate result of the defendant's wrongful conduct, Britt has suffered emotional distress, humiliation, loss of reputation, and other damages.

223. Defendants Bailey and Boone violated Ms. Britt's Fourth Amendment right to be secure in her

person, house, papers, and effects against unreasonable searches and seizures shall not be violated.

224. Defendants Bailey and Boone violated Ms. Britt's Fourth Amendment right to be secure in her person against unreasonable search when they used objectively unreasonable and excessive force during her arrest, "stating that the drug suspect in another vehicle had previously hidden drugs in a secret compartment on the car."

## NINTH CAUSE OF ACTION
### (North Carolina Constitution)

225. The allegations are incorporated by reference, as stated in all the paragraphs in this complaint.

226. The plaintiff alleged that the plaintiff's statement on August 29, 2023, was truthful and was compelled by the defendant's actions.

227. According to 42 U.S.C. § 1983, this claim was brought against defendants Gregg, Ketchie, Keith, Bailey, Skidmore, and Boone in their official and individual capacities.

228. The plaintiff states she made court appearances on January 9, 2023. January 10, 2023;

February and March 2023; and April 5, 2023. Also, on April 5, 2023, the plaintiff turned down the state's plea offer for the combination of probation violation and September 20, 2022, charges to be served concurrently in NCDAC.

229. The plaintiff states that on July 11, 2023, the plaintiff made an Application and Order For Limited Driving Privilege-Failure To Comply Revocation in Rockingham County, District Court Division Case File Number: 22CR 706225.

230. On July 13, 2023, Judge Christopher Freeman issued the plaintiff Limited Driving Privileges. The allowed driving hours were 12-4 pm and 11-7 am.

231. During court proceedings on July 13, 2023, the defendant entered the district court courtroom and saw the plaintiff sitting in the gallery; the defendant inquired by asking the prosecuting district attorney, "Why was the plaintiff in court?"

232. Once the defendant learned the plaintiff's reason, the defendant expressed her concerns to Judge Freeman why the plaintiff shouldn't be granted a limited driving license, and the defendant attempted to block the plaintiff's ability to receive

limited license privileges due to an open matter in superior court.

233. The court's ruling favored the plaintiff, stating the plaintiffs' superior court matters did not have any affiliation with the plaintiff's district court matters.

234. The plaintiff states she made court appearances on June 27, 2023, June 28, 2023, July 31, 2023, August 28, 2023, and August 29, 2023.

235. The plaintiff states that at the meeting she and her family held before the August 29, 2023, court appearance, she did not expect to receive an active sentence and be placed in the custody of the North Carolina Department of Adult Corrections due to the conversation on the day before.

236. During the meeting, the plaintiff and her family were told by Skidmore the following: "Her freedom depended on the testimony of my mother," "he would be using this 17 court appearance to have a free shot at the officers, as he was interested in what they'd have to say about the incident."

237. The plaintiff was convicted of probation violation charges, with an active sentence of 13-27 months, for Case Docket File No. 22 CRS 74. On

August 29, 2023, the plaintiff was placed in the North Carolina Department of Adult Corrections custody.

238. The plaintiff, of her own free will, requested to speak with the lead detective of an ongoing murder investigation. The plaintiff, of her own free will, provided law enforcement with vital information for an ongoing murder investigation.

239. The plaintiff states that the defendant has displayed unethical practices against her in this case. During the process of this case, the plaintiff stated that she asked to be contacted by the lead detective on an ongoing murder investigation to provide information on her free will and admission after witnessing the unethical practices that were conducted during the period of this case matter.

240. The plaintiff states that the defendants are obstructing justice by failing to accept responsibility for the misconduct of their Reidsville Police Officers during the September 20, 2022, traffic stop.

241. The plaintiff states the defendants are obstructing justice by failing to accept responsibility for the misconduct conducted by Rockingham County District Attorney Kathryn L. Gregg during court trial appearances on August 29, 2023, and

May 14, 2024, and by failing to prosecute the plaintiff's case matters to the full extent of the law to give disposition in the matter, and by failing to disposition of the plaintiff's case matter for receiving justice for the victim and the victim's families.

242. The plaintiff states that between October 2022 and May 2024, she observed the unethical practices committed against her while appearing in Rockingham County Superior Court Division, especially on "August 29, 2023" and with the newest complaint of unethical practices on May 14, 2024, in the matter of Caswell County Superior Court Division, Case File No. 24CRS 000042.

243. The plaintiff alleged that the plaintiff's statements on August 29, 2023, and May 14, 2024, were truthful and were compelled by the defendant's actions.

244. The plaintiff states that on May 14, 2024, the defendant appeared in Caswell County Superior Court at Judge Berlin's request. The judge wanted more information about the plaintiff's case before granting unsupervised probation.

245. The plaintiff states that on May 14, 2024, Judge Berlin made the following statement

regarding the status of the plaintiff's probation being transferred from supervised to unsupervised:

246. The plaintiff states that when she appeared before Judge Berlin without being in the presence of Kathy Gregg, Berlin, during the trial, said, "I do not mind letting you off probation and changing you over to unsupervised, but I don't want to do that, and then something happens, and they come back and violation you on the unsupervised, and this will have all been for nothing; I need more information about the matter before making a decision I need to speak with Kathy Gregg."

247. The plaintiff states that when she appeared before Judge Berlin without Kathy Gregg's presence, Berlin set a court continuation date in June 2024 during the trial. The plaintiff leaves Caswell County, Superior Court Division, under the impression the hearing was to be heard in the later parts of June.

248. The plaintiff states she left Caswell County Superior Court and returned to the residence of 691 Mineral Springs Road. Shortly afterward, the plaintiff said she received a call from the Clerk of Court in Caswell County asking her to return to court as they weren't finished with the case matter.

249. The plaintiff states that upon returning to Superior Court, the defendant was present for the court hearing. The defendant appeared at Judge Berlin's request. When the plaintiff's case was called, the defendant asked for the courtroom to be cleared.

250. The plaintiff states that upon returning to Superior Court, the defendant was present for the court hearing; the defendant provided false information to Judge Berlin to deny the plaintiff's motion to be transferred to unsupervised probation for the remainder of the plaintiff's probation term. The plaintiff states that the defendant was untruthful in her statement on May 14, 2024, about the contents of the Consent Order.

251. The plaintiff states that on May 14, 2024, the defendant's statement to Judge Berlin regarding the plaintiff's agreement with the state on October 6, 2023, per her release from the 19 NCDAC, as part of the Motion For Appropriate Relief agreement, the plaintiff was to follow the terms and conditions set forth for the reinstatement of the plaintiff's probation.

252. The plaintiff states that on May 14, 2024, the defendant's statement to Judge Berlin regarding the details of the Motion For Appropriate Relief

agreement was given verbally during trial court. The information provided by the defendant was the terms and conditions for the release on October 6, 2023, which the defendant considered untruthful in her statement.

253. The plaintiff states that on May 14, 2024, Judge Berlin asked the defendant, " Had she had a copy of the Motion For Appropriate Relief?" The defendant replied, "No, your honor, I do not, but I can pull it up on my phone."

254. The plaintiff states that Judge Berlin declined to see the Motion For Appropriate Relief via the defendant's cell phone.

255. The plaintiff states that on May 14, 2024, she tried to object to the court's requirement that she provide the correct filed and signed documentation of the terms and conditions regarding release on October 6, 2023.

256. The plaintiff states that during the court appearance, she objected to the statements that she had the correct documentation physically in hand against what the defendant was alleging: the terms and conditions of reinstatement of probation—the signed Motion For Appropriate Relief upon her

release on October 6, 2023—was not the most accurate document.

257. The plaintiff states that Judge Berlin refused to look at the physical copy of the plaintiff's documents to present to the courts; the plaintiff states she was denied her right to prove her innocence or defend the court right by Judge Berlin.

258. The plaintiff states that the untruthful statement given by Gregg on May 14, 2024, during a court trial in the Superior Court division of Caswell County—case File No. 24CRS 000042, was the primary basis for the denial of probation status change.

259. The defendant states the plaintiff was to have probation reinstated, details outlined in the Motion For Appropriate Relief, upon the willingness to follow the terms and conditions of Motion for Appropriate Relief, upon being 20 released, because defendant Gregg stated " she skipped out on a conviction sentence." and "she got herself out of a sentence by coming forward the day of conviction regarding an ongoing murder investigation."

260. The plaintiff states that the preceding paragraphs are incorporated by reference.

261. This claim is brought against defendants Kathryn Gregg, Kevin Ketchie, Christopher Bailey, Gregory Boone, Scott Skidmore, and Jason Keith in their official capacities.

262. The plaintiff states that the defendant revoked her probation term in retaliation for her official complaint against Reidsville Police Officers Chris Bailey and Greg Boone.

263. The plaintiff states that the defendant revoked her probation term in retaliation for her official complaint against Rockingham County District Attorney Kathryn Gregg.

264. The plaintiff states that the defendant revoked her probation term in retaliation for her official complaints against several members of law enforcement and by the defendant violating the plaintiff's United States Constitution's First Amendment, violating 42 U.S.C. § 1983.

265. The plaintiff states that once the plaintiff and her mother returned to Caswell County Superior Court when the plaintiff's case was recalled, the defendant asked the judge if the courtroom could be cleared. During the closed conference, the defendant testified to the following:

(1) The plaintiff agreed to the terms and conditions once the plaintiff was placed back on probation;

(2) If the plaintiff wanted to work out of the county, she needed to move there and speak about matters concerning the ongoing murder investigation.

266. The defendant was not truthful in her statement to Judge Berlin regarding the terms and conditions of the Consent Order signed at 10:45 a.m., October 6, 2023, by the late Honor Judge Stanley L. Allen versus the terms and conditions of the Motion For Appropriate Relief signed by only the plaintiff's attorney, Scott Skidmore, thirty (30) minutes before Judge Allen's Consent Order. 21

267. The defendant was not truthful in her statement to Judge Berlin regarding the late Judge Stanley L. Allen's refusal to accept the state's Motion For Appropriate Relief submitted by the plaintiff's attorney, Scott Skidmore, on October 6, 2023, at 10:15 a.m.

268. The plaintiff stated to the courts that the defendant did not have the correct documents, and the plaintiff had a physical copy that Judge Berlin

declined to review. The defendant was not truthful in her statement regarding the probation officer's ability to make or suggest decisions in the plaintiff's case matters; the judge left room for the probation officer's discretion. Judge Berlin did not allow P.O. William Brewer to speak on behalf of the plaintiff's motion to be placed on unsupervised probation.

269. Judge Berlin decided to deny it based on the defendant's statement. After the trial, Judge Berlin rejected the plaintiff's request to be transferred to unsupervised probation after the defendant's statement to the courts described the court findings of probation officer Kevin Ketchie used on August 29, 2023, to revoke the plaintiff's probation.

270. The plaintiff states that defendant Keith's description of the June 2, 2023 meeting was considered the premeditating practices used as described on August 29, 2023, court trial hearing for the probation violation hearing for case docket no. 22 CRS 74, with suspended sentencing of 13-27 months and a conviction from the September 20, 2022, traffic stop for driving while license revoked.

271. The plaintiff states that when the defendant presented its evidence to the courts on August 29, 2023, the defendant did not acknowledge the plaintiff's open complaints of NC State Bar Case

File Nos—23G0943 and 23G0944 against Kathryn L. Gregg and Jason Keith. The defendant's actions were those described in detail by Jason Keith.

272. The plaintiff states the defendant did precisely what Jason Keith described during the June 2, 2023, meeting with the plaintiff and her family. Keith's description also uses the same method to secure the conviction of probation violation for driving while license revoked. The same method is used to convict the 22 plaintiffs of probation violation for driving on a revoked license without the plaintiff being found guilty of charges accrued on September 20, 2022.

273. The plaintiff states that Jason Keith read aloud content that could be described as a premeditated sentencing. Via text message per Keith, the defendant said the following: "Mr. Keith, I know you're going to contest these drug charges, but let me tell you what I'm going to do;

274. I'm going to put the officers on the stand, and I'm going to have the officers say that she was driving without a license, not on the merits of whether she's guilty of the new charges or not; I will have the judge revoke her probation and send her to prison."

275. For all other times relevant above, the plaintiff states that at all times pertinent to the matter described above, the misconduct of law enforcement officers Bailey and Boone, unethical practices conducted by the Rockingham County District Attorney Office Officials, and attorneys Jason Keith and Scott Skidmore.

276. The plaintiff underscores that Britt endured emotional distress, humiliation, loss of reputation, and other damages as a direct consequence of the defendant's wrongful conduct, thereby establishing a clear link between the defendant's actions and the plaintiff's suffering.

## **PRAYER FOR RELIEF**

Based on the preceding, the plaintiff prays for the following relief:
1. That the Court declare that the defendant's practices complained of herein are unlawful under the United States Constitution and the North Carolina Constitution;

2. That the Court enter judgment in favor of the plaintiff and against the defendants for the plaintiff's emotional distress, public humiliation, loss of reputation, confined and false imprisonment, discrimination, and other compensatory damages in

the amount to be determined by a jury and interest as determined by the Court;

3.     That the Court enters a judgment in favor of the plaintiff to declare this filing a violation of her Constitutional Rights.

4.     The Court enters a judgment in favor of the plaintiff to release her from supervised probation and transfer her to an unsupervised status.

5.     The Court enters a judgment in favor of the plaintiff to possibly consider the expungement of criminal background histories of Ms. Britt and her mother, Latoye Britt.

6.     The Courts enter a judgment of $250,000 in damages, paid jointly and severally, by Bailey, Boone, Gregg, Keith, Ketchie, Skidmore, and Rockingham County Government, District Attorney.

7.     The Court entered judgment in favor of the plaintiff in the amount of $20,000 in damages from the Rockingham County District Attorney's office, Kathryn Gregg, for the personal vendetta behavior displayed and committed against Ms. Britt during the prosecution of the case file number 22CRS74.

8. That the Court enter judgment in favor of the plaintiff and against the defendants for punitive damages in an amount to be determined by a jury;

9. Ms. Britt also requests any additional damages in an amount determined by the jury, plus recovery of all costs of filing the lawsuit and preparation fees;

10. That the cost of this action be taxed against defendants;

11. The Court grants the plaintiffs trial by jury, and this Court deems such other and further legal documents filings and equitable relief as necessary, just, and proper.

## The Complaint II

The plaintiff states that Defendant Gregg was previously the prosecutor for driving charges in the lower court and a prior drug conviction in May 2022, placing the plaintiff on supervised probation for a term of 36 months. Defendant Gregg relied on the officers' accurate and complete information from their investigation, and Judge MeGee made a precise ruling based on that information. Defendant Gregg relied on the officers' accurate and complete information from their investigation, and Judge

Berlin made a precise ruling based on that information.

The plaintiff states that Defendant Gregg did not make a mistake during case matter 22CRS74. The plaintiff states that during case matter 22CRS74, Defendant Gregg displayed improper purposes while prosecuting the plaintiff's case and that Defendant Gregg prosecuted the matter maliciously. However, she was provided "fabricated" information by RPD officers Bailey and Boone, and she reasonably relied on that information to convict the plaintiff, knowing officers had "fabricated" this information.

The plaintiff states that Defendant Gregg instigated the criminal case as she displayed vendetta behaviors toward the plaintiff; she intended to convict the plaintiff by having officers commit perjury during their testimony at the plaintiff's trial.

RPD officers Chris Bailey and Gregory Boone conducted the traffic stop on September 20, 2022. The officers were found to have engaged in misconduct during the stop. The plaintiff states that although there was likely evidence to establish probable cause to believe the defendant committed the crime, that officers harassed, patterned," or' practiced, and targeted the plaintiff before, during, and after conducting its traffic stop on September 20, 2022. The plaintiff explained how she was initially detained, and an RPD officer issued a citation for driving and possession of crack cocaine. At the same time, the plaintiff's license was revoked. The arresting officer placed the driving citation in the plaintiff's mother's name. The plaintiff states that the prosecution harassed the defendant, ruined another person's reputation, and was actively involved in the plaintiff's original case.

The plaintiff states that, in the end, the Rockingham County magistrate, who issued the arrest warrant at the police officer's request, most likely would not have issued it if the officers had been more honest with their conduct at the traffic stop.

The plaintiff states that, most likely, the RPD officers would not have committed perjury during the trial if they had been more honest with their conduct during the traffic stop. The plaintiff states that the following September 20, 2022, traffic stop charges should have been disposed of once the plaintiff received certified documentation from the Internal Affairs Division of the Reidsville Police Department regarding the plaintiff's complaint of unethical practices committed against her.

The plaintiff concludes that after being convicted, found guilty of probation violation, and sentenced to 13-27 months, on October 6, 2023, at 10:15 a.m., the late Judge Stanley Allen rejected the terms and conditions "specially outlined" in the counsel's Motion for Appropriate Relief, prepared by the plaintiff's counsel. Judge Allen directed them to revise the terms and conditions and return to session promptly.

The plaintiff states that the District Attorney's Office is in conflict because it filed a complaint against the defendant before the trial hearing. The plaintiff states that before the trial, defendant Gregg was seen speaking with Officer Bailey; during the conversation, defendant Gregg could be heard whispering to Officer Bailey as well, and the plaintiff's family members were able to read the defendant's lips during the conversation.

The plaintiff alleges that defendant Gregg coached Officer Bailey on his testimony. Once Officer Bailey took the stand, defendant Gregg asked, "Did you or Didn't you see Ashley Britt get in or out of the car?" The plaintiff states that Defendant Gregg has displayed a vendetta against her in more ways than one throughout the prosecution of this case.

Furthermore, the plaintiff concludes that after being convicted, found guilty of probation violation, and sentenced to 13-27 months, on October 6, 2023, at 10:45 a.m., the late Judge Stanley Allen signed a Consent Order regarding the plaintiff case matter while presiding Judge Allen "specially outlined" the terms and conditions of the Consent Order upon the plaintiff's release. During this session on October 6, 2023, Judge Allen ordered the plaintiff to be released from the Rockingham County Detention Center and not transported back to the North Carolina Department of Corrections.

## The Amended Complaint

IN THE UNITED STATES DISTRICT COURT FOR THE MIDDLE DISTRICT OF NORTH CAROLINA GREENSBORO DIVISION

ASHLEY DESEIRAY BRITT,
Plaintiffs,
v.
KATHRYN LEBAUBE GREGG et al.
Defendants.

THE PLAINTIFFS' MOTION TO AMEND AND SUPPLEMENT THE COMPLAINT

[Plaintiff] motion to amend its complaint contains the following allegations: On July 30, 2024,

[Plaintiff] met with Attorney Scott Skidmore concerning the upcoming court appearance for the pending charges that occurred on September 20, 2022. [Plaintiff] was sitting in the waiting area of Mr. Skidmore's office in Reidsville, North Carolina. During the wait, [Plaintiff] overheard a phone conversation between District Attorney Kathryn Gregg and Mr. Skidmore.

[Plaintiff] could hear DA Gregg state, "She doesn't feel I should get the plea arrangement. "She didn't feel I deserved it." [Plaintiff] could hear Mr. Skidmore state, "Regardless of whether you like it, my client isn't going back to jail or prison. So we're going to get her to plead guilty and not to revoke her probation and give her six (6) months, then give her unsupervised probation in October or November no later than December, as long as she doesn't get into any more trouble."

During the conversation, [Plaintiff] says the phone conversation became so intense that Mr. Skidmore raised his voice, which caused other members present in the office to come from inside their office spaces.

[Plaintiff] decided to record this meeting with Mr. Skidmore concerning the conversation she'd just overheard concerning her, the disposition of this case matter, and the misconduct and unethical practices committed by Rockingham County District Attorney Kathyrn L. Gregg.

[Plaintiff] did not feel confident about the words that may have or would have been stated during the meeting. For [Plaintiff] safety, [Plaintiff] records on her cell phone. A copy of the conversation is also provided via USB.

## STATEMENT OF FACTS

[Plaintiff] filed a complaint against the defendant, alleging that she had engaged in unprofessional conduct. While employed as an Assistant District Attorney and as the District Attorney of Caswell & Rockingham County Prosecutorial District 22. The defendant assisted with false statements about the plaintiff to secure a conviction in August 2023 with individuals who provided a public service to residents of Rockingham County and the City of Reidsville, North Carolina.

The defendant used her public servants to misrepresent the existence of evidence to the presiding judge during a trial and for engaging in a conflict of interest and conduct prejudicial to the administration of justice. The facts are taken from the stipulations submitted by the [plaintiff's] original Complaint filed on June 13, 2024 [plaintiff] is a woman who was placed on probation on May 22, 2022, for a term of three (3) years, with a suspended sentence to a minimum term of no less than thirteen (13) months and no more than twenty-five (25) months.

On August 7, 2024, [Plaintiff] accepted the plea of supervised probation for a term of 24 months with a suspended sentence of six (6) to seventeen (17) months. [Plaintiff] probation term if to be supervised under William Brewer. With expectations of being transferred to unsupervised around November or December.

## **BACKGROUND**

During the court appearances on August 29, 2023, and May 14, 2023, Defendant knew the statements made by herself, Bailey, Boone, and Ketchie were false statements given to the courts, making them all violate the Rules of Professional Conduct. This causes the revocation of probation and an active sentence of 13 to 25 months. October 6, 2023, Honorable Stanley Allen signed a Consent Order releasing [Plaintiff] from the North Carolina Department of Adult Corrections.

On May 14, 2024, the Defendant knew the information given to the Courts concerning the terms and conditions was inaccurate. This information was incorrect; the defendant told the Courts that [Plaintiff] had agreed to the terms and conditions under the Motion of Appropriate Relief, and somehow [Plaintiff] got herself out of a prison sentence." Along with [Plaintiff], [Plaintiff] was being held on probation because she was the witness for a murder investigation.

On August 7, 2024, [Plaintiff ] appeared in Rockingham County Superior Court to accept the plea offer of 24 months, suspended by 6 to 17 months, Case Docket Number 22CRS300093, due to the September 20, 2022, traffic stop.

## IN CONCLUSION,

The plaintiff believes the defendant has been abusing her power as the District Attorney for Prosecutorial District 22: Caswell and Rockingham Counties concerning the Court's actions and behaviors in the case of this matter. This action arises from the plaintiff's amended complaint to reflect the critical dates, such as June 2, 2023, August 29, 2023, and May 14, 2024. Defendants knew those statements to have been given under Oath that were false statements given to the courts, making them all in violation of the Rules of Professional Conduct. However, the Defendant is entitled to immunity as an elected state official.

Her actions in this matter weren't to help the good of Rockingham County but to abuse her authority as the Then-Assistant District Attorney and now District Attorney for Caswell and Rockingham Counties, Prosecutorial District 22.

The actions displayed by Defendant throughout this court proceeding and trial matters were actively engaged to confirm the words spoken by Jason Keith on June 2, 2023, to [Plaintiff's] mother. "I don't know whether you know this, but Katy Gregg has it out for your daughter." This was followed by Mr. Keith reading aloud a text message sent by Defendant via phone, the plan the defendant described in detail as to how she would send the [Plaintiff] to jail.

Defendant has displayed her feelings toward [Plaintiff] more than once, indicating a personal vendetta she has acquired toward the plaintiff. She stated, "[Plaintiff] continues to get in trouble, and [Plaintiff] has not done anything positive while being on probation." The defendant's vendetta revolved around her personal feelings for her thoughts as she felt [Plaintiff] was continuously getting in trouble. Defendant's actions toward [Plaintiff] were malicious, willful, wantonly, or in a manner that demonstrates a reckless disregard for Plaintiff's rights, eventually ending on August 7, 2024, with a plea trial.

In the last conversation overheard on July 30, 2024, between Mr. Skidmore and the defendant, the defendant once again displayed her personal feelings regarding this case and the disposition. The Defendant said, "She doesn't feel I should get the plea arrangement. "She didn't feel I deserved it." She displayed a personal vendetta instead of applying the law in this case.

Based on the previous, the plaintiff prays for the following relief:

That the Court declare that the defendant's practices complained of herein are unlawful under the United States Constitution, the public policy of North Carolina, and the North Carolina Constitution;

That the Court enter judgment in favor of the plaintiff and against the defendant for the plaintiff's emotional distress, humiliation, loss of enjoyment of life, and loss of reputation by providing the Plaintiff with a written or voiced public apology;

The Court should enter judgment in favor of Plaintiff and against the defendant for Plaintiff's criminal record to be erased with the Court's consideration for the inconvenience the matter has caused.

That the Court enter judgment in favor of Plaintiff and against the defendant for the Plaintiff's mother, La Toye Britt's criminal record to be erased with the Court's consideration as she's a victim in the matter.; Such other relief as this Court deems necessary, just, and proper.

These amendments will not prejudice defendants as the added information arises from the same operative facts previously pleaded in the complaint. The plaintiff is raising these claims before discovery has been completed. The plaintiff admits the newly added documents represent other factual elements concerning the complaint.

WHEREFORE, the Plaintiffs respectfully ask that the Court grant the Plaintiffs to amend the Complaint their Amended Complaint and for such other relief as the Court deems just and proper.

Dated: August 8, 2024, Respectfully Submitted,

**Caswell County Sheriff Office**

IN THE UNITED STATES DISTRICT COURT FOR THE
MIDDLE DISTRICT OF NORTH CAROLINA
GREENSBORO DIVISION

TYLAN DELSHAUN THAXTON, TALAISHA DAYSHAUN THAXTON, and LATOYE ANN BRITT,
Plaintiffs,

v.

CASWELL COUNTY SHERIFF TONY DURDEN JR, his Official capacities, OTIS FOSTER, Official capacities, KEN MITCHELL in his individual and Official capacities, and JOHN DOE CORPORATION, in its capacity as Surety on the Official Bond of the Sheriff of Caswell County,
Defendants.

**COMES NOW** the Plaintiffs, Tylan Thaxton, Talaisha Thaxton, and Latoye Britt, Pro Se, as Representative in the Complaint against Defendants Tony Durden Jr., in his official capacity as Sheriff of Caswell County, North Carolina. Otis Foster, in his official capacity as Administration Major of Caswell County, North Carolina, and Kenneth Mitchell, in his individual and official capacities as Lieutenant of Investigations Division, Caswell County, North Carolina. The Plaintiffs, with an unyielding resolve, are steadfast in their pursuit of justice for violating their rights.

## **PARTIES**

1. Tylan Thaxton, plaintiff, is a citizen and resident of Caswell County, North Carolina.

2. Talaisha Thaxton, plaintiff, is a citizen and resident of Caswell County.

3. LaToye Britt, plaintiff, is a citizen and resident of Caswell County, North Carolina.

4. Defendant County of Caswell (after this "Caswell") is a municipal corporation located in Caswell County and organized under the laws of the State of North Carolina.

5. Caswell County Sheriff's Department, as the Defendant, bears the utmost responsibility for the policies, practices, and customs of its Sheriff Department, which are currently under scrutiny in this complaint. This legal document underlines the weight of their actions.

6. Defendant Otis Foster, an administrative employee with the Caswell County Sheriff's Department, is being sued in his capacity as Major Operations. It is crucial to note that he acted within the scope of his employment and under the color of law at all relevant times relevant to the material incidents in this complaint, thereby amplifying the gravity of the situation.

7. Defendant Ken Mitchell, an administration employee with the Caswell County Sheriff's Department, is being sued in his capacity as an Investigation Lieutenant. It is crucial to note that he acted within the scope of his employment and under the color of law at all relevant times relevant to the material incidents in this complaint, thereby amplifying the gravity of the situation.

8. The CCSO office's primary duty is to safeguard lives and property and protect the innocent from becoming victims of deception and oppression while always respecting our citizens' constitutional rights.

9. Defendant Tony Durden Jr. has been the duly elected Sheriff of Caswell County, North Carolina, since 2017.

10. Durden has final policy-making authority for CCSO and extends to personal decisions. It is crucial to note that at all times relevant to the material incidents in this complaint, he acted within the scope of his employment and under the color of law, thereby amplifying the gravity of the situation. He's been sued in his individual and official capacities.

11. Defendant Durden is to represent the County of Caswell with integrity and professionalism while protecting victims and their rights in pursuing justice. At all times pertinent to the material incidents in this complaint, he acted within the scope of her employment and under color of law, further emphasizing the seriousness of the situation.

12. Defendant Joe Doe Corporation is a make-believe name for the Surety of the Official Bond of defendant Durden, Jr as Sheriff of Caswell County, according to N.C. Gen. Stat § 162-8 and § 58-76-5, whose identity is presently unknown to the plaintiff. The actual name will be made to this claim once it is revealed.

13. Upon information and belief, the defendant is insured by one or more liability insurance policies purchased according to N.C. Gen. Stat. § 153A-435 or other applicable state law for all acts and omissions complained of herein or participated in a government risk pool according to N.C. Gen. Stat. § 58-23-5, or maintains a funded reserve. To such extent, the defendant has waived any official, sovereign, qualified, or government immunity to which he might otherwise be entitled in his official capacity.

**JURISDICTION, VENUE, AND NOTICE**

14. Plaintiff repeats, re-alleges, and re-asserts each allegation outlined in the preceding paragraphs as if fully set forth herein.

15. This action arises under the Constitution and laws of the United States, including Article III, Section 1 of the United States Constitution and 42 U.S.C. § 1983 and 42 U.S.C. § 1988.

16. The court has jurisdiction according to 28 U.S.C. §1343(3) (civil rights) and 28 U.S.C. §1331 (federal question).

17. This case is instituted in the United States District Court for the Middle District of North Carolina, according to 28 U.S.C. §1391, as the judicial district where all relevant events and omissions occurred and where the Defendants maintain offices or reside.

18. Supplemental pendant jurisdiction is based on 28 U.S.C. §1367 because the violations of federal law alleged are substantial, and the pendant causes of action derive from a common nucleus of operative facts.

19. This Court also has jurisdiction under the Declaratory Judgment Act, 28 U.S.C. §§ 2201–02.12.

20. This claim also arises under the common law and the Constitution of the State of North Carolina. This Court has original jurisdiction over the plaintiff's state law claims according to 28 U.S.C. § 1367.

21. Almost all material events giving rise to this cause of action occurred in Caswell County, North Carolina. Based on information and belief, defendant Tony Durden resided in Caswell County.

22. Almost all material events giving rise to this case of action occurred in Caswell County, North Carolina. Based on information and belief, defendant Otis Foster resided in Caswell County.

23. Almost all material events giving rise to this cause of action occurred in Caswell County, North Carolina. Based on information belief, defendant Ken Mitchell resided in Caswell County. The proper venue is the Middle District Court of North Carolina. Under 28 U.S.C. §§ 1391(b).

24. The venue is proper in the U.S. District Court for the Middle District of North Carolina under 28 U.S.C. § 1391(b)(2) because a substantial part of the acts that gave rise to this lawsuit occurred in this judicial district. This district is also

an appropriate venue under 28 U.S.C. § 1391(b)(1) because defendants reside in this judicial district.

## BACKGROUND

25. Plaintiff repeats, re-alleges, and re-asserts each allegation outlined in the preceding paragraphs as if fully set forth herein.

26. Caswell County Jail was established in 1885, shortly after the formation of Caswell County in 1777. The original jail was a log cabin located in the county seat of Yanceyville. It served as the primary detention facility for the county until the construction of a new prison in the 1960s. The Administrative Division is responsible for all data entry, sexual offender registration, gun permits, concealed weapon permits, domestic violence orders, and fingerprinting of criminal and non-criminal individuals.

27. The Records Division maintains incident and arrest reports and assists with information for Deputies, insurance companies, and the public. The sheriff is the chief law enforcement officer of the county. Dawson v. Radewicz and Southern Railway Co. v. Mecklenburg County

28. The National Sheriffs' Association is a U.S. trade association. Its stated purpose is to raise the level of professionalism among U.S. sheriffs, their deputies, and others in the fields of criminal justice and public safety.

29. The North Carolina Sheriffs' Education and Training Standards Commission is responsible for certifying all justice officers, including deputy sheriffs, detention officers, and telecommunicators, who are employed in the 100 Sheriffs' Offices in this state, according to N.C.G.S. 17E.

30. On his website, Defendant Sheriff Durden represents the Caswell County Sheriff's Office and believes in all people's dignity and worth. We must safeguard lives and property, protect the innocent from becoming victims of deception and oppression, and always respect the constitutional rights of our citizens.

31. The Caswell County Sheriff's Office Investigations Division is responsible for criminal investigations throughout Caswell County and is generally accountable for felony investigations. The Division is a separate unit providing specialized and complex investigative techniques, including crime scene investigations. The Investigations Division encompasses the following areas: Property Crimes

include, but are not limited to, felony theft, felony breaking, and fraud. Crimes against Persons include but are not limited to, kidnapping, sexual assault, homicides, robberies, and felonious assault.

32. Defendant Sheriff Durden has the full legal authority and responsibility for operating the Caswell County Sheriff's Department. Defendant Sheriff Durden delegates the responsibility for operations of the Caswell County Sheriff's Office to the Administrator of Major Operations, Defendant Otis, at all times, which is material hereto. Defendant Sheriff Durden has the full legal authority and responsibility for operating the Caswell County Sheriff's Department.

33. Defendant Sheriff Durden delegates the responsibility for operations of the Caswell County Sheriff's Office to the Administrator of Investigation Services, Defendant Mitchell, at all times, which is material hereto.

34. They were willfully Failing to Discharge the Duties of the Sheriff's Office N.C. Gen. Stat. § 14-230 makes it unlawful for a sheriff to "willfully omit, neglect or refuse to discharge any of the duties of his office."

35. N.C. Gen. Stat. § 153A-103. Number of Employees in Offices of Sheriff and Register of Deeds The text of N.C. Gen. Stat. § 153A-103- 1. Each sheriff has "the exclusive right to hire, discharge, and supervise the employees" in the sheriff's office.

36. Sheriff Durden is officially sued under G.S. 58-76-5 and G.S. 153A-435. He and his office are also sued according to the Doctrine of Respondeat Superior for the actions and omissions of his Officers, employees, servants, and agents.

37. Defendant Sheriff Durden has waived any claim of sovereign immunity for himself, his deputies, servant, and employees by purchasing a surety bond according to N.C.G.S. 58-76-5 or by buying liability insurance according to N.G.S. 153A-435 or by participation in a risk management pool as authorized by statute, thereby waiving any governmental or sovereign immunity that might otherwise apply to the Sheriff or his agents in this action.

38. Defendant, Operations Major: Major Otis Foster (in the future referred to as "Defendant Foster"), to Plaintiff's information and belief, is a citizen and resident of Caswell County, North Carolina, and was at all material times employed by

Sheriff Durden at the Caswell County Sheriff Office and is being named as a Defendant herein in his capacity.

39. The surety bond and the commercial insurance or risk pool arrangement referred to in the previous paragraph waive any claim to governmental or sovereign immunity that Defendant might claim in his official capacity.

40. Defendant, Investigation Division Administration: Lieutenant Kenneth Mitchell (in the future referred to as "Defendant Mitchell"), to Plaintiff's information and belief, is a citizen and resident of Caswell County, North Carolina, and was at all material times employed by Sheriff Durden at the Caswell County Sheriff Office and is being named as a Defendant herein in his capacity.

41. The surety bond and the commercial insurance or risk pool arrangement referred to in the previous paragraph waive any claim to governmental or sovereign immunity that Defendant might claim in his official capacity.

## **INTRODUCTION**

Plaintiff repeats, re-alleges, and re-asserts each allegation outlined in the preceding paragraphs as if fully set forth herein.

42. On his website, Defendant Sheriff Durden represents the Caswell County Sheriff's Office and believes in all people's dignity and worth. We must safeguard lives and property, protect the innocent from becoming victims of deception and oppression, and always respect the constitutional rights of our citizens.

43. The Caswell County Sheriff's Office Investigations Division is responsible for criminal investigations throughout Caswell County and is generally accountable for felony investigations. The Division is a separate unit providing specialized and complex investigative techniques, including crime scene investigations. The Investigations Division encompasses the following areas: Property Crimes include, but are not limited to, felony theft, felony breaking, and fraud. Crimes against Persons include but are not limited to, kidnapping, sexual assault, homicides, robberies, and felonious assault.

44. Defendant Sheriff Durden has the full legal authority and responsibility for operating the Caswell County Sheriff's Department. Defendant Sheriff Durden delegates the responsibility for

operations of the Caswell County Sheriff's Office to the Administrator of Major Operations, Defendant Otis, at all times, which is material hereto.

45. Defendant Sheriff Durden has the full legal authority and responsibility for operating the Caswell County Sheriff's Department. Defendant Sheriff Durden delegates the responsibility for operations of the Caswell County Sheriff's Office to the Administrator of Investigation Services, Defendant Mitchell, at all times, which is material hereto.

46. The North Carolina Sheriffs' Education and Training Standards Commission is responsible for certifying all justice officers, including deputy sheriffs, detention officers, and telecommunicators, who are employed in the 100 Sheriffs' Offices in this state, according to N.C.G.S. 17E.

47. Common Law Duties and Authorities of the Office of Sheriff The common law remains in "full force and effect" in North Carolina unless legislatively changed. Thus, the sheriff's typical law duties are still the law and duties of the sheriff unless altered by statute.

48. Duties such as jail operation, law enforcement, service of process, and courts

(bailiffs) existed in common law and have not been changed by statute in North Carolina. The General Statutes explicitly codify some of these duties and assume the existence of others.

49. In March 2021, Tylan Thaxton and his sister, Tashaun Thaxton, were involved in a dispute between Thaxton's sister and the girlfriend of a coworker who was said to have been in a secret relationship with Thaxton's sister.

50. TaShaun was physically working at Pelican Healthcare Nursing and Rehabilitation when she observed her co-worker's girlfriend vandalizing her vehicle.

51. The coworker's girlfriend drove to their place of employment. She physically damaged Thaxton's vehicle by throwing coffee on her windshield, kicking and spitting on the car, and using her bumper to hit TaShaun's vehicle in the parking lot. TaShaun called Tylan and told him of the incident. For about 20 minutes, both parties chased one another through Reidsville.

52. The coworker and girlfriend proceeded to head toward Caswell County, taking Highway 158 East. While they were in pursuit of one another,

Tylan Thaxton stuck a gun out the window and fired 2 to 3 shots in the air.

53.     Leading to an ending on US HWY 158 East; during this chase, Thaxton DID shoot into the air, while GF reported when she called 911, he shot at her vehicle while he was chasing her.

54.     Shortly after the call to 911 communications, the coworker and girlfriend were pulled over by CCSO deputies. CCSO deputies spoke with them, and then they were permitted to leave. Deputies headed towards Thaxton's parked vehicles.

55.     As they parked and watched the deputies, their vehicles faced the opposite direction: TaShaun facing the highway and Tylan's facing the opposite direction.

56.     They were both sitting inside TaShaun's car when deputies approached it. They stated that a CCSO (Blk) approached TaShaun's vehicle, and the officer then asked for ownership of the car. Neither of the Thaxtons answered his question. The officer ran TaShaun's tag number; her name had a pick-up tag status attached to it.

57. As the deputy was walking toward the rear of TaShaun's vehicle, he also instructed TaShaun to get out and tried to gain entry by opening the driver's side door. However, the driver's door was jammed and could not be opened.

58. Tylan first removed himself so TaShaun could cross over to the passenger seat to gain exit from the vehicle. When she got out of the car, deputies placed her in handcuffs and searched her car, only to find an open container, which was disposed of by the officer who'd put the handcuffs on her.

59. When asked why her vehicle was being searched, the officer replied that he had the right to do that because there was an order to pick up her license.

60. Since neither party involved had identified their vehicles with the authorities, we assumed that it was when officers ran the tags. His sister was placed in the back of the patrol car.

61. Thaxton was handcuffed as soon as he exited his sister's vehicle. He had been placed in the investigator's before they searched his car. Thaxton acknowledges that he did NOT permit CCSOs to search his vehicle.

62. During the search, it was discovered Mr. Thaxton had money, weed, and a gun. Money and weed were found inside his car, while the weapon was found on the inside of his pants leg.

63. The CCSO conducted a gunpowder residue test at the scene. Did indeed give Thaxton a gunpowder residue test at the scene of the incident. This is very important for future actions of the CCSO gunpowder residue test.

64. Thaxton was placed into custody and taken to CCSO for processing. We waited for him to be given a bond for almost four hours. As a result of the lengthy time frame, it was brought to our attention that CCSO officers were trying to process Mr. Thaxton with charges that were inexcusable to the magistrate on duty.

65. After waiting five hours or more, Mr. Thaxton was finally given a secured bond of $5,000. Upon his release, items retrieved during the search were kept from Mr. Thaxton.

66. However, he was able to provide documentation to account for the amount of money recovered during the search. Those funds weren't returned.

67. Mr. Thaxton accepted the plea for the gun instead of the drugs, and we believe that after receiving this plea and learning the severity of the situation, Thaxton felt as if the CCSO was harassing him.

68. The defendant's actions were done maliciously, willfully, wantonly, or in a manner that demonstrates reckless disregard for Thaxton's and Britt's rights. As a result of the defendant's conduct, the plaintiff is entitled to recover punitive damages. As a proximate result of the defendant's wrongful conduct, Thaxton and Britt have suffered emotional distress, humiliation, loss of reputation, and other damages.

69. The defendant's actions were maliciously, willfully, wantonly, or in a manner that demonstrates reckless disregard for the plaintiff's rights by canvasing the plaintiff's property without permission.

70. The North Carolina Constitution protected the plaintiff's freedom. There was no legitimate, non-discriminatory reason for CCSO deputies to canvas a citizen's property without prior authorization.

71. The concerns expressed by the plaintiff on more than one occasion were regarding unethical practices, personal feelings, vendetta, and misconduct shown toward the plaintiffs.

## **FIRST CAUSE OF ACTION:**

Plaintiff repeats, re-alleges, and re-asserts each allegation outlined in the preceding paragraphs as if fully set forth herein.

72. May 15-25, 2022: The first initial visit to my residence was without probable cause. When deputies arrived, no one announced themselves as CCSO, and no one came to knock at the door. Deputies could be observed writing down license plate information for parked vehicles at the residence.

73. Deputies were observed walking around the plaintiff's property. Deputies walked to the back of the property, where the utility building is located. While deputies were at the rear of the property, they could be observed looking through the windows of the plaintiff's utility building. One deputy attempted to open the utility door until another deputy stopped him.

74. During the times in question, deputies were unaware someone was inside the residence; they were being watched from inside the residence. After deputies proceeded to walk around and record information, they knocked on the door; when the person inside the residence answered the door, CCSO was asked, "Why were they walking around the property without someone knowing they were out there?"

75. Deputies were not expecting someone to answer the knock; once the person inside opened the door and asked "why they were freely walking the property without first speaking with someone," deputies at that moment asked if Tylan was home.

76. Deputies were asked again," Why were they walking around the property without speaking with someone or knocking on the door first?" At this point, deputies became rude and started harassing the person inside, asking questions regarding the vehicles and a dirt bike leaning against a pole on the side of the plaintiff's deck.

77. Deputies were interested in the dirt bike at the front of the property. During the word exchange, the person on the inside expressed several times that he was not the homeowner and could not speak with them. He asked again why they walked around the

property without announcing themselves when they first entered.

78. Deputies were unaware that the homeowner, Ms. Britt, could listen to the events happening at the residence during this time as she was video chatting with someone inside the home.

79. Ms. Britt could hear deputies tell the person to "make sure the dirt bike doesn't move." "make sure that dirt bike stays there until we come back."

80. Ms. Britt could hear deputies tell the person, "Shouldn't be answering doors if he doesn't live there."

81. While Ms. Britt was on the video call, deputies were unaware that Ms. Britt could hear them and that they were rude and disrespectful to the person inside her home.

81. Since Ms. Britt was absent, she called her daughter, Akia Mills, to pick her up and bring her to the residence. In transit to the home, Ms. Britt called the CCSO non-emergency line several times to complain about the deputies' unethical behaviors while on the property.

82. While on the phone, Ms. Britt continuously asked the sheriff's department for those same

officers to return to the residence and asked for the names and badge numbers of the deputies involved in the incident.

83. Ms. Britt expressed several times the wrongdoing of the deputies on her property without her presence. Ms. Britt said it was wrong for deputies to treat and speak to the guests at her home rudely and discourteously.

84. Ms. Britt expressed her horror at deputies threatening the person at her house, telling her not to move the dirt bike from its location as they would be coming back for it.

85. Due to the events, Ms. Britt called and left several messages for someone to explain why those officers conducted themselves as they did. Ms. Britt called CCSO several times to speak with someone about the deputies' misconduct at the residence.

86. Ms. Britt spoke with Capt. Loftis concerning the matter. Capt. Loftis also expressed his concern about how deputies may have handled the situation differently than the way they did.

87. During Ms. Britt's conversation with Capt. Lotfis, Loftis, told Ms. Britt, "He was going to see about some type of classes or something similar."

At that time, I was informed that K. Roberts would be the detective on the cause, and I needed to refer all questions to him because he was the lead detective on the case.

88. As informed, Ms. Britt has yet to speak with K. Roberts concerning the matter from the day of the incident until this Complaint. At that moment, the conversation ended because Ms. Britt was told to wait until K. Roberts contacted her.

89. Ms. Britt called several more days later, inquiring about the same information. When Ms. Britt asked about it, Ms. Britt was told, "Someone else would be handling the matter. K. Roberts was unavailable; he had a family emergency.

90. Ms. Britt, at the time of this Complaint, still has not spoken with K. Roberts concerning the misconduct of CCSO deputies when they were at Ms. Britt's residence.

91. At the time of this Complaint, Ms. Britt will compare the search warrant issues at the residence on two separate incidents, essential and referenced in the Jan. 23rd and 24th, 2023 incidents.

## **SECOND CAUSE FOR ACTION:**

Plaintiff repeats, re-alleges, and re-asserts each allegation outlined in the preceding paragraphs as if fully set forth herein.

92. On or about May 22nd-23rd of 2022, Ms. Britt received a call from Lt. Callhaun. Lt. Callhaun connected with Ms. Britt, asking if she was home.

93. Lt. Callhaun asked Ms. Britt if she could meet CCSO at the residence. They had a search warrant for Ms. Britt's utility building at the back of the home.

94. Lt. Callhaun stated, "He wanted to call me so I could be there because he did NOT want an incident like before." I agreed to come and give permission for CCSO to search the utility building Located at the back of the home.

95. When Ms. Britt arrived, she was greeted by Lt. Callhaun. Lt. Callhaun explained to Ms. Britt that Lt. Mitchell would be conducting the search and handling the case.

96. When Ms. Britt inquired why K. Roberts was no longer involved in this case matter. She was told the case was handed off to Lt. Mitchell.

97. Lt. Mitchell and deputies were at Ms. Britt's residence for over four hours in the utility building, trying to determine whether the dirt bikes inside the building were the bikes they were searching for.

98. During the building search, Ms. Britt told Lt. Mitchell where the stolen dirt bikes could be located; Ms. Britt also provided Lt. Mitchell with the names of the individuals who had possession of the stolen bikes at the time of the search.

99. The information provided by Ms. Britt to CCSO's Lt. Mitchell on the day of the search was not investigated.

100. Ms. Britt states that at the time of this complaint, the information given on the day of the search still needs to be investigated. As to Ms. Britt's understanding, there have been more reports of stolen dirt bikes in the area after this incident.

101. Lt. Mitchell was still looking at the photos to see if this was the dirt bike they were searching for. After thirty to forty minutes of Lt. Mitchell examining photos, Ms. Britt called Tylan Thaxton via video chat via Facebook messenger.

102. Tylan explained over the phone to Lt. Mitchell where his parts come from and provided

receipts for when someone purchased another dirt bike for him and where he brought all types of accessories and gear. CCSO's Lt. Mitchell and deputies knew this before leaving the residence.

103. During the search, Lt. Mitchell kept glancing and messing with his phone. When Ms. Britt asked why the search took so long, Lt. Mitchell, the lead detective, stated that he was trying to communicate with the victim. He was unsure if this was the correct bike and whether either bike in Ms. Britt's building was the bike in question.

104. Once, Lt. Mitchell said he was trying to ask the victim if this was the right bike, but he could not send messages due to an insufficient signal. At Ms. Britt's residence, a Wi-Fi signal is needed to communicate and use cellular devices.

105. Ms. Britt informed Lt. Mitchell of the signal information and offered to take Lt. Mitchell's phone and connect it to the Wi-Fi.

106. Lt. Mitchell stated he could not give me the victim's phone. Although Lt. Mitchell stated he could not provide Ms. Britt with the victim's phone, Lt. Mitchell still proceeded to give Ms. Britt the victim's phone.

107. At this time, Ms. Britt took possession of the victim's phone from Lt. Mitchell. Ms. Britt walked to the back of the home, went up the steps, and entered the back door into her kitchen.

108. As Ms. Britt connected the victim's phone to the Wi-fi, Ms. Britt could see the phone number associated with the phone. While Ms. Britt had the victim's phone in her possession, she did not look through the device.

109. Ms. Britt turned around and walked back out the door and down the steps. Once outside, Ms. Britt returned the victim's phone to Lt. Mitchell.

110. Lt. Mitchell then proceeded to go back into the building. At this time, Ms. Britt left the back of the home where the search was being conducted, went inside the residence, and video-called Tylan Thaxton again.

111. While on the video call with Tylan, Ms. Britt gave him the number she remembered from when she had the phone from Lt. Mitchell.

112. During the conversation with Tylan, he told Ms. Britt to enter the number into the Cash app, which would reveal who the number was registered to.

113. Ms. Britt and Tylan Thaxon could determine that Lt. Mitchell and the victim were related. Ms. Britt stated that the Cash App revealed that the phone was registered with Jayden Mitchell.

114. Ms. Britt states Lt. Mitchell's involvement in the case causes a conflict of interest. Lt. Mitchell is related to the individual, Jayden Mitchell.

115. Ms. Britt states that once she received this information, she returned to the search being conducted and told Lt. Mitchell that if they were not going to take anything from her home, they needed to leave the premises.

## **THIRD CAUSE OF ACTION:**

Plaintiff repeats, re-alleges, and re-asserts each allegation outlined in the preceding paragraphs as if fully set forth herein.

116. Ms. Britt says that before deputies came to her residence with the search warrant, which happened around the same time, CCSO deputies came to Ms. Britt's residence for nonsense calls and the harassment of Tylan Thaxton. All the while, CCSO deputies canvassed the property.

117. Days before the search, Tylan rode his dirt bike on Mineral Springs Road. While riding, he observed a vehicle following behind him, driving at an unusual speed. After Tylan noticed the car, he could begin to ride alongside it. Tylan observed Lt. Mitchell, a female occupant, and someone seated in the back of the rental vehicle.

118. Ms. Britt submitted a Complaint to the CCSO, Sheriff Tony Durden, regarding this incident and was able to provide photos of the same dirt bike, which Lt. Mitchell stated was stolen.

119. Ms. Britt states that at the time of his Complaint, the CCSO had not contacted Ms. Britt or Tylan and Talaisha Thaxton regarding the contents of the Complaint.

120. Ms. Britt states that within the next few days of Tylan riding alongside the rented vehicle, two friends of Jayden visited Ms. Britt's residence. In return, Jayden's friends told Jayden his dirt bike was at Tylan Thaxton's house.

121. Officers walked around my property the next day, slightly jarring my shed door open to look in. The officers did not know someone was in my house looking at them through the back window.

122. Officers were bullying my guest and repeating to him, "Make sure that dirt bike stays right there. You're going to jail, buddy". This is when I called about how they conducted themselves and why they did NOT wait until I got to the residence. That call should be recorded as well.

123. Jayden Mitchell's paying and offering to pay individuals for the address, communicating threats through social media, and being related to the leading investigator create many conflicts of interest.

124. Ms. Britt states she has text messages and social media posts from Jayden's friends, proof that Jayden Mitchell offered to pay an individual for Ms. Britt's address.

125. Ms. Britt states she has text messages and social media posts from Jayden's friends, proof that Jayden Mitchell paid an individual for Ms. Britt's address.

## **FOURTH CAUSE OF ACTION:**

Plaintiff repeats, re-alleges, and re-asserts each allegation outlined in the preceding paragraphs as if fully set forth herein.

126. Ms. Britt states that in the months leading to the January 23rd, 2023, incident, CCSO has been to her residence at least ten to twelve times in response to the neighbor, neighbors, repeatedly calling CCSO complaining of Ms. Britt's kids running through and on her property.

127. Ms. Britt states that in the months leading to the January 23rd, 2023, incident. CCSO has been to her residence at least ten to twelve times in response to the neighbor, neighbors, repeatedly calling CCSO and complaining of Ms. Britt's kids riding their dirt bikes through and on her property.

128. Ms. Britt states that in the months leading to the January 23rd, 2023, incident, CCSO visited her residence at least ten to twelve times in response to the neighbor.

129. Neighbors called CCSO complaining of Ms. Britt's kids running through and shooting on her property.

130. Ms. Britt states the following concerns and issues described below were addressed in a complaint previously submitted to the CCSO.

131. Ms. Britt states she has not been given any information regarding the complaint against Sheriff

Durden, Major O. Foster, and Lt. Mitchell, submitted in late 2023.

132. Ms. Britt stated her complaint against Sheriff Durden, Major O. Foster, and Lt. Mitchell, submitted in 2023 to CCSO the following:

133. Ms. Britt's residence was shot into, and her home was shot into by the same individuals she'd previously identified to Lt. Mitchell during the day of the search in May in the hot weather.

134. Ms. Britt called CCSO to complain about the neighbor, who at the time lived across from Sheriff Durden on Mineral Springs Road. The neighbor physically came to Ms. Britt's residence, communicating threats to kill one of her dogs due to one of his pits being killed. No one from the CCSO came to investigate the matter.

135. On the day the first neighbor threatened Ms. Britt, she went to a second neighbor's home. This neighbor does live behind Sheriff Tony Durden.

136. Ms. Britt went to the second neighbor's home because, at the time, this neighbor had a black dog named Big Boy, who belonged to the neighbor's sister and lived across the road from the Sheriff.

137. Ms. Britt only knew this information about Big Boy's owner because she and the neighbor had spoken before when Big Boy first started coming to Ms. Britt's home.

138. Ms. Britt went to the second neighbor's home to inform him of the first neighbor's intentions of saying he was going to shoot the dogs.

139. Ms. Britt had called several times before the first neighbors commented on killing the dogs. Ms. Britt called CCSO and the animal shelter to discuss the treatment of the animals, especially during the summer months. Ms. Britt complained about the dogs not being fed and not being provided water during the summer.

140. Ms. Britt had called several times before the first neighbors commented on killing the dogs. Ms. Britt called CCSO and the animal shelter to discuss the treatment of the animals, especially during the summer months.

141. Ms. Britt complained about the location of the training and fighting equipment with the animals and about their lack of protection in the winter.

142. No one from CCSO, Ms. Britt, ever came to check Ms. Britt's complaints. At the end of this incident, Ms. Britt's pit bull and Shih Tzu were shot by the first neighbor.

**FIFTH CAUSE OF ACTION:**

Plaintiff repeats, re-alleges, and re-asserts each allegation outlined in the preceding paragraphs as if fully set forth herein.

153. In January, Ms. Britt wrote to Sheriff Durden: "January 23, 2023: I'm genuinely not trying to be one of those parents trying to seek justice after the fact- it's my discretion that CCSO conducted some of these procedures unethically.

154. Things like coming onto my property without announcing themselves could have been deadly. They would not know someone was inside the residence and would freely walk around on someone's property without permission or any indication of why they were there.

155. My location was 11 miles and 15 minutes from 691 Mineral Springs Rd. Tylan picked me up around 2:20-2:30 p.m. We returned around 4:45 p.m.

156. I'm optimistic about this time. I need to confirm an appointment time for the following day. My phone was off, and I needed Tylan to call the doctor to confirm the time.

157. When he helped me in the house, I looked at my calendar, where I thought I had written it down, but I did not. I asked what time it was. We both looked and saw that it was 4:45 p.m. I told my son there was still enough time for him to call them for me, get confirmation, and text me back through the Wi-Fi.

158. At 5:45 p.m., Tylan texted me asking if I could help him pay a bill. I replied to Him at 5:53 p.m. After this, I didn't contact Him again until 9:36 p.m. According to the Caswell County news release, this happened at 7:30 p.m.

159. The reported CCSO time is off, according to the CCSO news release. Suspect Thomas, on the night in question, left the scene, returned to the scene, and began to shoot on Mineral Springs Road.

160. Suspect Thomas alleged the home on Mineral Springs Road, where shots were fired at the house located on Mineral Springs Road, the home of Anita Graves, thinking it was the home of Mr. Thaxton.

161. On this same night, the shooting occurred. Suspect Thomas is believed to have driven to Raleigh-Durham International Airport for a flight departing RDU and arriving at LAX. This same night, J.T. left the scene, came back, and shot up the Graves residence, thinking it was ours. I proceeded to RDU to catch a flight to LAX the same night. This is the baseline for this situation.

162. Both Thaxtons can give more in-depth details from that night. I have the following information on what happened that night: January 23, 2023. Those detained were K'Shawn Farrish (17), Ace (19), and Sosa (20).

163. The only one I knew to be there was K. Farrish. So here's the storyline from earlier in the day leading up to 9:36 p.m. At 9:36 p.m., Tylan didn't answer his phone, so I called his sister.

164. That call was at 9:38 p.m. When I spoke with Talaisha, I asked her what she was doing. She told me she was in the kitchen washing dishes, and they were cleaning up.

165. So I asked who was there, who were they? Talaisha said it was her, one of my granddaughters, and another female (between ages 15 and 17). I

asked her who was there twice, and she repeated the same.

166. I asked her if the police were there because I had received a call that they were hiding in the woods behind my house. My daughter advised me that there weren't any police at my house then.

167. 9:26 pm-I received a call about the Caswell County Sheriff dept. I had surrounded my residence from 9:36-38 pm- where I stated above, where I called my daughter-also during this time, after hanging up with my daughter, I called my son to see where he was to tell him about the phone call.

168. I needed him to go home to check on his sister (she was pregnant). At 10:30 pm, I received a text from my son asking me to call him. During this call, we tried to figure out what had happened and why the sheriff had surrounded my home.

169. I got off the phone with my son at that time. The next call I received was from my daughter at 11:37 pm.

170. At 11:37 p.m., deputies arrived at my residence. When I answered the phone, she was yelling, and they bum-rushed down my driveway to my front door, about 5 to 7 police cars 2.

171. During this call, I spoke with Chief Foster. I asked him why they were at my residence. He first told me the scent of gunpowder led them to my residence.

172. He also told me they were looking for three individuals involved in a shooting on Mineral Springs Road. This is when I told him I was tired of everything in that area; it always had to be my son.

173. I told them I was tired of them coming to my residence for my son. I told him they shouldn't be there and that my son had nothing to do with what had happened.

174. During this call, he advised me that they would stay on my property until they received a search warrant, and my reply was that it was late and that I needed to come out to permit them to search my residence.

175. It was later revealed to my son & me that an ex-employee of CCSO stated that Durden permitted them that night to enter my residence due to the continuous harassment calls being placed by our neighbor Anita Graves.

176. When I visited Durden the following day, he assured me this search was performed correctly.

177. My daughter repeated every word, so they knew I was not coming to permit them. (The search warrant and permission are due to an issue with another case; I will explain the comparison at that point).

178. I also told him not to get the castings already in my yard confused with the casting from this shooting. While being detained, she experienced unnecessary roughness (she's pregnant).

179. Also, while being detained, she explained and expressed how her body was exposed because there were male officers in her presence, and she was naked.

180. When I mentioned this situation to Durden as a concern, he responded, "He didn't care what happened as long as there was a female officer present."

181. My daughter's body was fully uncovered-she had just taken a shower. (Durden, when I mentioned this the following day, he told me it was none of his concern as long as a female officer was present.

182. Everyone in my household was detained that night by CCSO. This shooting involved three

individuals I did not know of by the neighbors calling and reporting my son shot up their home.

183. Which indeed prompted CCSO to visit my residence once again. Three of the individuals were later found and eventually charged with shooting inside an occupied dwelling from the guns in the safe that was located in the residence.

184. Two weeks later, CCSO came back with warrants for both of the Thaxton twins for felony possession of a stolen firearm.

185. CCSO did a news break with my home when neighbors said that Tylan and the small boys were the ones that shot up their house and ran back into the woods towards my residence.

186. It was very embarrassing, considering all parties were detained, none of which was Tylan. At that moment, I wasn't aware that three individuals had been found in my residence.

187. It wasn't until the following morning, when I canceled my doctor's appointment to go to the sheriff's office to speak with the Sheriff about the prior night's events, that I found out about the three young men."

188. Gunpowder Residue Testing Onsite During the residence search, CCSO detained three individuals who were considered suspects in this shooting.

189. These three individuals who were in custody never gave a gun residue testing on the spot. vs. when my son was accused of shooting while he was driving, he did admit to firing in the air, not at the vehicle.

190. Driving on the highway- he was charged; he had a gun, but he was given the gun residue testing on the spot. Why wasn't this handled in the same fashion as March 2021? The residence was surrounded by law enforcement. No one administered the gunpowder residue testing.

191. Per the search warrant, they were looking for any evidence leading to or associated with shooting into an occupied dwelling. Once receiving the warrant, my daughter told me how the deputies unlawfully entered my residence.

192. As a guest at my residence, a 16-17-year-old African American female was greeted by a deputy of CCSO.

193. The deputy had already assisted himself in entering my residence without executing the search

warrant for the homeowner or announcing himself the correct way.

194. (Through their admission, they stated they didn't want a situation like the last one regarding the search warrant but didn't follow the same protocol this time.)

195. I knew the last known disagreement with the Graves was around the second to the third week of January. Mr. and Mrs. Graves have had problems with my children before, as they told the deputies on occasion. Mr. and Mrs. Graves said, "It was my son shooting at their residence."

196. They called because he was riding his dirt bike through the path. This elderly couple called the police on my son because he was riding his dirt bike, so there's history.

197. I have also enclosed a copy of my property lines. They reported shots fired, and the report said she was in her bedroom.

198. When I met with the chief and the sheriff the following morning, he stated that " they were in the living room, and bullets went right by their heads."

199. She ran and looked out her back door and saw the individuals running toward my residence.

200. One of the most important things mentioned while in their presence was why they blamed my son.

201. My son wasn't even present, nor was he one of the three detained when they had a news break airing cops surrounding my residence with an active shooter.

202. May I add three hours after the shooting? CCSO said approximately 7:30 p.m., but that time frame isn't correct. This occurred between 6 pm and 6:45 pm.

203. There's an individual who spends a lot of time in my woods located in the back of the residence, and this is mainly because when I called for patrol about the neighbor who keeps his dogs at his grandmother's home on a piece of my property, no one ever responded to my complaints.

204. This is how we can know about some of the behaviors displayed by CCSOs. All of the shooters have been apprehended. None of the three individuals was my son. Tylan DelShaun Thaxton

wasn't responsible for the shooting, as they were proclaiming, as Tylan and I were together.

205. I have mailed copies of this information to the local Law Enforcement Officials, CCSO, the Civil Rights Department, and the Department of Justice.

## **SIXTH CAUSE OF ACTION:**

Plaintiff repeats, re-alleges, and re-asserts each allegation outlined in the preceding paragraphs as if fully set forth herein.

206. Failure to Intervene: an officer who purposefully allows a fellow officer to violate a victim's constitutional right may be prosecuted for failure to intervene to stop the constitutional violation.

207. To prosecute such an officer, the government must show that the defendant officer was aware of the constitutional violation, had an opportunity to intervene, and chose not to do so.

208. This charge is often appropriate for supervisory officers who observe uses of excessive force without stopping them or actively encourage

uses of excessive force but do not directly participate in them.

209. Major O. Foster allowed Durden to use an excessive tone of voice for almost two minutes as he stood up and spoke very loudly to get my house in order and for me to leave his office.

210. I listened and observed Durden become verbally abusive during the conversation because I disagreed with my son being responsible. As I described, he became more outraged when I said you blamed this on my son.

211. Observing how Durden allowed his emotions & feelings to become involved with this case because he was going after the charge of attempted murder of his neighbors.

212. Observing Durden's behavior toward me, his attitude, temperament, demeanor, and personal feelings, Foster never interrupted until Durden stood up yelling at me, telling me to clean my house and get my house in order while telling me to get out of his office.

213. I was not wanted for questioning. I went to the sheriff's department seeking answers about the night before events. I went there to inquire about

my residence because I-We feel like our rights have been violated.

214. I told Durden I would have my son call CCSO with the information he knew about this incident, which my son did. I told Durden I would NOT bring him there for them to arrest him. I'd have him call them, and that's what we did.

215. Our actions and behaviors are based on the fact that we feel Tylan is a victim of a pattern or practice for these law officials in Caswell County.

216. Due to the strength of our family, we're there for one another as a family. If it were not for us, CCSO would have never caught those shooters, especially the one from Reidsville.

217. I feel it's a shame I must and need to take these measures to protect my son due to the rumors of his reputation among the neighbors, the sheriff, and the officers. He's only been convicted of one charge.

218. I honestly, once again, don't want to be another African-American female begging for justice for my son or burying him at anyone's expense. Tyan absconded for almost (1) a year and a

half, and Tony Durden stayed across the street from us.

219. Sheriff has told me several times before how he's spoken with Tylan about the shooting on our property.

220. The sheriff has also been to the residence to talk with Tylan about the dirt bikes riding due to a conflict with the neighbors (neighbors of us both) for being on their property when. Indeed, it's still my property line that she states belongs to her.

221. The point of all this is that if Tylan was wanted and committed all these crimes, why was it so hard for law enforcement to get him, and he was right across the street the whole time?

222. Current pending charges: Ty'Lan D' Thaxton Caswell & Rockingham Counties: Case Number: 22CR050196 Felony-Breaking and Entering, Felony, Larceny after Breaking; Month and Year-May 2022-Caswell County Issues: False Arrest—False arrest involves illegal searches and seizures, which are protected by the Fourth Amendment and controlled by the Constitution. An officer can be proven responsible in a police brutality lawsuit if they lack probable cause to

believe that the accused had committed a crime or was in the process of committing a crime.

223. Conflict of interest- Investigating Detective Lt. Mitchell relates to the victim Jayden Mitchell as a parent, grandparent, aunt/uncle, or cousin. Investigator Mitchell provided the victim's phone to the house owner while searching a utility building at 691 Mineral Springs Road in Pelham, NC.

224. The cell phone number was recognized as Jayden Mitchell's. Jayden Mitchell and Ty'Lan Thaxton had completed business transactions in the past.

225. Investigating Detective Lt. Mitchell, a female occupant, and Jayden Mitchell were seen in Mineral Springs looking for Thaxton's physical address. This conversation can be verified.

226. Jayden Mitchell contacted a friend of his and Thaxton's via text message. Jayden Mitchell texted for this information in cash to retrieve Thaxton's physical address. It can also be verified that Jayden Mitchell offered payment for this information in the form of money.

227. Investigating Detective Lt. Mitchell was observed by Thaxton on Mineral Springs while

riding alongside the vehicle on another ATV before executing the search warrant in May of 2022.

228. It can be verified that CCSO deputies visited Thaxton's home a few days before being served a search warrant for the outside utility building.

229. These five to six deputies were present during this visit. A family member inside the home observed the actions and behaviors of CCSO deputies: deputies did not announce themselves when first coming onto the property and did not knock on the door to see if anyone was inside the home.

230. CCSO deputies searched the property without a warrant, took pictures, and wrote down vehicle information.

231. Deputies were also observed walking to the rear portion of the property and looking into the utility building.

232. One deputy is observed opening the door of the utility building, one deputy is observed looking into the windows of the utility building, and one deputy is observed walking behind the utility building.

233. The utility building, a potential site of interest in this case, has never been locked as long as it has been located in the rear of the property. The deputies were observed returning to the front of the property and by a family member inside the home.

234. Once CCSO deputies noticed him, they became aggressive, harassed him, and were very disrespectful and rude. A complaint was made on behalf of these deputies regarding their actions and behaviors that day.

235. The homeowner called the CCSO several times, complaining about the treatment given by the deputies, threatening comments made by the deputies, and the unethical practices of the deputies on that day. Singling out a dirt bike prompt on the side of the deck, one officer stated, "Make sure this dirt bike is here when we come back."

236. After several calls by the homeowner requesting those same officers return to the residence, complaints ranged from not announcing themselves once they were on the property to the unethical practices seen performed (deputies were unaware a person was inside the residence) and being caught on surveillance video surrounding the property.

237. Around 1:30 p.m., the homeowner received a call from CCSO apologizing for the deputies' actions and behaviors. This call was placed by either Callhaun or Logan.

238. During this conversation, she was advised that a detective named Keith or Kevin Roberts would handle this report and contact me later to answer any questions concerning the incident.

239. While holding this conversation, the homeowner was asked what she would like to see happen with these officers, and it was explained how dangerous it was for the deputies to walk around someone else's property freely. This could have been a severe issue. Someone could have died because the deputies just felt comfortable walking around someone else's property, canvassing the property unlawfully.

240. The homeowner stated that these deputies might need to return for a refresher course in basic training or an educational course to perform. However, the homeowner was merely stating her opinion. The bottom line she wanted to express was these deputies' unethical practices in May 2022.

241. A few days later, the homeowner called CCSO, hoping to speak with the investigating

detective. At this time, it was stated he wasn't available to talk with the homeowner due to having an emergency. The homeowner was told to return a call the following week.

242. On a second attempt the following week, believed to be Monday morning, the homeowner called CCSO in hopes of speaking with the investigating detective. During this conversation, the homeowner was told that this detective could not reach her due to illness.

243. Later in the week, Lt. Callhaun of CCSO contacted the homeowner. Lt. Callhaun explained there was a search warrant for the utility building on the property. Could she come to the residence so they could execute the warrant? He stated, "He wanted to know how long it would take her to get there.

244. He was providing a call because he did not like the same situation as before, but it was agreed upon as she headed to the property. When arriving, the homeowner was introduced to Lt. Mitchell, who was now investigating this case.

245. The homeowner asked about what happened with the detective assigned to the case. At this time, it was stated again that Roberts was out due to an

illness. Lt. Callhaun left the property, and Lt. Mitchell started to search the building.

246. He explained what he was looking for, as they had been on the property for at least three hours. Mitchell did not have an identification from the victim stating that it was indeed the bike. Lt. Mitchell spoke with Thaxton via Facebook.

247. Thaxton was listed as an absconder for probation violation. Lt. Mitchell stated, "I know he (Thaxton) has other things going on with the law, but if you could get him on the phone, that would be great."

248. Before contacting Thaxton, the homeowner called his daughter's mother to verify that she had just purchased a bike for Thaxton. He provided receipts for the motorcycle, parts, and accessories and showed them to Mitchell while searching.

248. Lt. Mitchell also spoke with Thaxton's daughter's mother, who told Lt. Mitchell, "She purchased the bike and drove to the location to retrieve it. Thaxton provided information about how he obtained such items and receipts showing where he bought them 250. Thaxton provided each person and place where any dealings were made regarding any dirt bike on the property. As others on

the property observed, we believe Lt. Mitchell wasn't concerned with those receipts.

249. Lt. Mitchell was still determining if this was indeed the correct dirt bike. Lt. Mitchell decided this was the correct bike due to a particular cutting located on the riding seat of the bike.

250. But they should have disclosed that two other seats were cut like the one he retrieved. Those seats were also present inside the building but were not taken in as evidence in the matter.

251. Investigating Detective Lt. Mitchell removed a dirt bike from the property, still unsure whether or not this was indeed the dirt bike in question of the crime.

252. He stated, "If this were not the bike, he would return the bike. Since this time, the bike has been sold.

253. He was improperly investigating the thief of his relatives' property. As stated above, the victim, Jayden Mitchell, is somehow related to Lt. Mitchell by either cousin, father, grandfather, or uncle. As of November 6, 2023, this matter still needs to be resolved.

254. The statement from one of the individuals detained on January 23, 2023, is also provided. Since then, he has been on an electronic monitor, and there is no reason for such monitoring for his release in this matter.

255. After several court appearances, this still hasn't been resolved. K. Farrish. Sheriff Durden has tried to communicate with Ms. Thaxton, sister, knowing she has an attorney.

256. She was approached during the first appearance, which was reported to her attorney. Her attorney stated she needed proof that this would be a he-say/she-say situation.

257. As you will read in the information provided, Sheriff Durden used various communication methods to speak with Ms. Thaxton about this situation.

258. Deputies searching for information about an attempted murder suspect in Caswell Co. The Caswell County Sheriff's Office is looking for the person or people responsible for firing shots into a home on Mineral Springs Road.

259. On January 23, 2023, the Caswell County Sheriff's Office responded to a call of shots fired

into an occupied dwelling on Mineral Springs Road in the Pelham community. Anyone with any information on this incident is asked to contact the Sheriff's Office at 33-694-2555 or the Caswell County Crime Stopper at 336-694-5199.

260. Firearm Suspect Arrested: Caswell County Sheriff's Office- Pelham, NC. Plaintiff Tylan Thaxton was arrested and charged with a FELONIOUS criminal offense (1) count of POSSESSION OF A STOLEN FIREARM. He was placed in Caswell County Detention Center under a $ 50,000 SECURED BOND. His first appearance in Caswell District Court is scheduled for Wednesday, February 22nd, 2023, at 9:00 am.

261. Ta'Laisha D. Thaxton Caswell County-12/13/2023 Case Number: 23CR00031 C5179189-Misdemeanor-RESISTING PUBLIC OFFICER Case Number: 23CR225372 Felony-POSSESS STOLEN FIREARM On Jan. 23rd, our home located at 691 Mineral Springs Road in Pelham, NC was searched by CCSO about a drive-by shooting.

262. During this search, each party in the residence was detained by CCSO while being detained, and no one was given any residue testing,

nor was anyone arrested. A safe was removed from the residence.

263. Upon entry to the safe, two weapons were recovered. About 2 to 3 weeks later, Kashawn Farrish (my child's father) was charged with a shooting crime related to this incident.

264. The CCSO detained Farrish from her residence, stating there was a juvenile petition to bring him into custody. However, the CCSO did not provide an arrest warrant to detain Mr. Farrish.

265. He was detained from February 3rd until March 3rd. Without providing any paperwork for his detention, his probation officer was not informed that he was in custody, and they attempted to question him without a parent present.

266. On March 3rd, Farrish was sent home with the home monitoring device. Farrish's first appearance was toward the end of March, and I was present with him at this appearance.

267. During this appearance, Durden approached me. He said, "I know you didn't have anything to do with this, but we charged you because you live there." I told him, "I have an attorney and can't talk

to you without his presence." After this, I contacted my attorney to inform him.

268. Despite his knowledge of my legal representation, Durden's persistent attempts to communicate with me are a matter of concern. He was even present for my first court appearance.

269. After speaking with the attorney, I was informed that this was mostly his word against mine type of situation. If he were to put Durden on the stand, this would be his first encounter with him since being charged with felony possession of a stolen firearm, and my twin was accused of the same crime.

270. On Aug. 10th, 2023. I was in Food Lion around 6:45 pm-7:00 pm. I was standing on the candy aisle looking for "original" Hot-Chews. Durden came on the aisle as well.

271. He saw me and said, "Hey, how are you?" "I said I'm good, how about you?" Then he said, "Oh, you already had the baby?" "I said, yes, I had him six weeks ago." This was the end of the conversation.

272. Durden walked away and asked the person stocking where he could find a Sprite with no

caffeine. The stocker told him the next aisle, and Durden left the aisle. I was walking up to come off the aisle when my phone rang. It was my sister who was asking me what I was doing. "I said to the food lion, looking for some "original" Hot-Chews 'cause they are hard to find.

273. We talked, and I told her, "Tomorrow, I have to go to the courthouse and get a package for Mama. " She asked me, "What kind of? "I stated, "I don't know. It's just a package. I will ask her again tomorrow what kind before I go." I was still on the phone, walking up the aisle. Again, I was greeted by Sheriff Durden.

274. Sheriff Durden told me, "You must go to the police department tomorrow." I said, "Yes, I have to pick up a packet for my mom." He said, "Well, can you meet me at my office at 1 p.m.?" I said, "Yes, but I have an attorney." I agreed to meet with him so he could stop talking to me.

275. Before leaving Food Lion, I inboxed my mother and inboxed in our family group chat, as we all still said he spoke with you. Like before, my mother told me to write down the date, day, and time of anything dealing with CCSO.

276. After a prior conversation with Sheriff Durden, Ms. Thaxton agreed to meet Sheriff Durden at the CCSO on August 11th, 2023.

277. CCSO on August 11th, 2023. I did not meet with Sheriff Durden on the specified date and time, as I'd previously agreed to. I did not meet with the Sheriff at the agreed-upon time. As a result of not meeting Sheriff Durden on the scheduled date and time agreed upon, Sheriff Durden called my mother.

278. I did not meet with Durden at the agreed-upon time. Durden called my mother's number, looking for me. Sheriff Durden called 336-514-8751 from the CCSO phone number 336-694-9311 at 1:10 p.m. but didn't get Ms. Thaxton.

279. Then, at 1:37 p.m., Sheriff Durden called 336-514-8751 from his cell phone. His cell phone number used at the time of this Complaint registered to Sheriff Tony Durden, Jr., is 336-514-5124.

280. As Durden knows, I have an attorney who couldn't speak with me, but he attempted again, making me wonder why K. Farrish still had to be held for a crime for which the CCSO has no proof he was involved.

281. His fingerprints were not found on any weapon, and there was no gun residue- he wasn't tested even though he was detained, as they stated they were looking for an active shooter.

282. Today, August 25, 2023, Farrish is still on the home monitor device without an explanation. His fingerprints were not found on anything, and he was one of the persons detained on the night of this incident.

283. As of August 22, 2023, Farrish was told in court he would remain on house arrest until his next court appearance in February 2024.

284. The persons involved in this incident have already been arrested, charged, bonded, and waiting to appear in court. A metal safe (not listed in SW) was taken from the seizure, along with anything dealing with a firearm, bullets, holsters, etc., including the search warrant. CCSO was able to recover two handguns from the metal safe that were not listed as an item on the search warrant.

285. This was discovered after the safe was removed. Neither my brother nor my fingerprints were found on either weapon, and it was then discovered that one of the guns had been stolen from Burlington.

286. As I stated above, during Farrish's court appearance in March, Durden said, "I know that you didn't have anything to do with this, but we charged you with it because you live there." This was the statement stated by Sheriff Tony Durden of CCSO.

287. Deputies searching for information about an attempted murder suspect in Caswell Co. The Caswell County Sheriff's Office is looking for the person or people responsible for firing shots into a home on Mineral Springs Road. On January 23, 2023, the Caswell County Sheriff's Office responded to a call of shots fired into an occupied dwelling on Mineral Springs Road in the Pelham community. If anyone has any information on this incident, you are asked to contact the Sheriff's Office at 336-694-2555 or Caswell County Crime Stopper at 336-694-5199.

288. Shooting Suspect Arrested: Person County Sheriff's Office- Roxboro, NC. Aaron Tsaddio Ward was served with a Caswell County FELONY WARRANT FOR ARREST, charging him with (1) count of DISCHARGING A WEAPON INTO OCCUPIED PROPERTY. He was released from Person County Detention Center after posting a $25,000.00 SECURED BOND. His first appearance in Caswell District Court is scheduled for Wednesday, March 15th, 2023, at 9:00 am.

289. Shooting Suspect Arrested: Caswell County Sheriff's Office arrested and charged Yanceyville Township NC resident Immanuel Xavier Anderson with the commission of the following FELONIOUS criminal offenses: (1) count of DISCHARGING A WEAPON INTO OCCUPIED PROPERTY. He was released from the Caswell County Detention Center after posting a substantial $20,000.00 SECURED BOND. His first appearance in Caswell Superior Court is scheduled for Monday, March 13th, 2023, at 9:00 am

290. Shooting Suspect Arrested: Caswell County Sheriff's Office arrested and charged Reidsville, NC resident Jomonica Lenaye Thomas with the commission of the following FELONIOUS criminal offenses: (1) count of DISCHARGING A WEAPON INTO AN OCCUPIED DWELLING. She was released from the Caswell County Detention Center after posting a $10,000.00 SECURED BOND. Her first appearance in Caswell Superior Court is scheduled for Wednesday, April 5, 2023, at 9:00 am.

291. Shooting Suspect Arrested: Person County Sheriff's Office- Roxboro, NC. Aaron Tsaddiu Ward; Shooting Suspect Arrested Immanuel Xavier Anderson; and Shooting Suspect Arrested: Jomonica Lenaye Thomas were arrested and

charged with line number 287. Line numbers 287-290 were published via the CCSO website, providing information to the public in regards to the January 23, 2023, shooting on Mineral Springs Road, Pelham, NC 27311.

## SEVENTH CAUSE OF ACTION:

Plaintiff repeats, re-alleges, and re-asserts each allegation outlined in the preceding paragraphs as if fully set forth herein.

292. Police misconduct involves unethical and unlawful activities by law enforcement officials, including excessive force and unreasonable searches and seizures.

293. Reputation of the involved officers: An officer's history of police misconduct and other government officials—violates the plaintiff's constitutional rights. Police Misconduct and Civil Rights Violations—Police swore to serve and protect the community.

294. Wrongful Search and Seizure: CCSO deputies interrogated and searched the Thaxtons based on "reasonable suspicion" and unfairly targeted the Thaxtons, which made this search and seizure unconstitutional. Plaintiffs are protected

from wrongful search and seizure by the Fourth Amendment. However, CCSO overstepped its bounds.

295. Unlawful Arrests: CCSO arrested the Thaxtons based on "reasonable suspicion." After the information and details surrounding the matter, the Thaxtons were victims of illegal arrests without legal grounds. The plaintiff states this has occurred due to unfair profiling and abuse of power. Unlawful arrests can ruin people's lives.

296. CCSO arrested the Thaxtons based on "reasonable suspicion." After the information and details surrounding the matter, the Thaxtons were victims of unlawful arrests without legal grounds and malicious prosecution. The plaintiff states this has occurred due to unfair profiling and abuse of power.

297. The Thaxtons are entitled to Freedom of speech, religion, and assembly; freedom from discrimination; the right to procedural due process; and the right to petition the government.

298. CCSO's Major Otis Foster witnessed CCSO's Sheriff Durden violating the civil rights belonging to Ms. Britt on January 24, 2023, when she contacted the CCSO regarding her children,

Tylan and Talaisha Thaxton. Major O. Foster failed to prevent or stop this violation from occurring.

299. Police misconduct settlements have a history of being substantial. These claims have four essential components: initiating a criminal legal proceeding without probable cause, with malice, and a judgment in favor of the victim. We ask the courts to make a settlement, including stipulated reforms on how police warrants are handled.

300. Before Tylan and Talaisha Thaxton's arrest, Tylan's first encounter with the CCSO was in March 2012. While Talaisha Thaxton has not had an encounter with the CCSO, other community citizens have observed the exact behavior of the CCSO.

301. The defendants' CCSO policies described above indicate that they have engaged in a pattern and practice of Constitutional and Civil Rights law violations at the Caswell County Sheriff's Office.

302. With a direct and proximate result of the aforesaid constitutional violations, civil rights violations, and misconduct of Defendants, jointly and severally, the Plaintiff has sustained damages in an amount over Two-Hundred Fifty Thousand and No/100 Dollars ($250,000.00), ($75,000 per plaintiff), including for pain and suffering of Tylan

and Talaisha Thaxton, and Latoye Britt before their arrest and all misconduct of CCSO Law Enforcement.

303. Defendants' acts and omissions were the legal and proximate cause of violations of Tylan Thaxton and Talaisha Thaxton's Federal and State Constitutional Rights.

304. At all relevant times, Defendants CCSO were acting under color of State law, had in effect express or de facto policies, practices, procedures, and customs that were a direct and proximate cause of the wrongful, unconstitutional, and unlawful conduct of CCSO officers and other law officials involved worked at Caswell County Sheriff Office.

## PRAYER FOR RELIEF

WHEREFORE, plaintiffs Tylan Thaxton, Talaiaha Thaxton, and Latoye Britt pray the Court to enter a judgment and award against Defendants, jointly and severally, as follows: practices complained of herein are unlawful under the United States Constitution and the North Carolina Constitution;

That Plaintiff has and recover of the Defendants, jointly and severally, compensatory damages in an amount over SeventyFive Thousand and No/100

Dollars ($75,000.00) for damages, together with interest at the legal rate; pray the Court to enter a judgment and award against Defendants, jointly and severally, as follows:

1. Respectfully asks that the Court enter judgment in favor of the plaintiff and against the defendants for the plaintiff's emotional distress, public humiliation, loss of reputation, confined and false imprisonment, discrimination, and other compensatory damages in the amount to be determined by a jury and interest as determined by the Court;

2. Respectfully asks that the cost of this action be taxed against the defendants and with any other filing fees regarding the Complaint;

3. Respectfully asks that the Court enter judgment in favor of the plaintiff and against the defendants for punitive damages in an amount to be determined by a jury;

4. Respectfully asks that the Court grant the plaintiffs trial by a jury and

5. Respectfully ask that immediate relief be taken into consideration for the plaintiff's inability

to obtain gainful employment with consideration of record expungement;

6. Respectfully asks that the Court consider granting the plaintiffs immediate relief. The plaintiff asks for such relief due to the pending charges hindering the plaintiffs from moving forward with their lives.

7. Respectfully asks that the Court consider granting the plaintiffs access to receive additional education, including but not limited to admission, books, and tuition fees, as this Court deems necessary that is just and proper.

8. Respectfully that such other and further legal documents filings and equitable relief as this Court deems necessary that is just and proper.

### Caswell County Sheriff Office II

Current pending charges: Ty'Lan D' Thaxton Caswell & Rockingham Counties: Case Number: 22CR050196 Felony-BREAKING AND OR ENTERING Felony-LARCENY AFTER BREAK/ENTER Month and Year-May 2022-Caswell County Issues: Can a detective investigate a crime, if the detective is related to the victim in any way?

    1. They can, especially in a small department, initially, but most Chiefs or

Sheriffs will assign the case to another officer or deputy or to another agency to work on. That ensures the officer does not influence the case.

2. Not usually, as this will be a conflict of interest. It's not likely the officer will be able to remain impartial and professional, as it's obviously personal, so this will cloud their professional judgment.

Conflict of interest—Investigating Detective Lt. Mitchell is related to the victim, Jayden Mitchell, as a parent, grandparent, aunt/uncle, or cousin. Investigator Mitchell provided the victim's phone to the house owner during a search of a utility building located at 691 Mineral Springs Road in Pelham, NC.

The cell phone number was recognized as Jayden Mitchell. Jayden Mitchell & Ty'Lan Thaxton had completed business transactions in the past. Investigating Detective Lt. Mitchell, a female occupant, and Jayden Mitchell were seen on Mineral Springs looking for Thaxton's physical address. This conversation can be verified. Jayden Mitchell contacted a friend of his and Thaxton's. Jayden Mitchell's method of communication was by text message.

Jayden Mitchell texted this associate, inquiring and trying to retrieve Thaxton's physical address. It can also be verified that Jayden Mitchell offered payment in the form of money for this information. Investigating Detective Lt. Mitchell was observed by Thaxton on Mineral Springs as he was riding alongside the vehicle on another ATV. Before executing the search warrant in May of 2022, it can be verified that deputies of CCSO visited Thaxton's home a few days prior to having been served a search warrant for the outside utility building.

There were at least five to six deputies during this visit. The actions and behaviors of CCSO deputies observed by a family member inside the home watching are as follows: deputies did not announce themselves when first coming onto the property, deputies did not knock on the door to see if anyone was inside the home.

CCSO deputies also did the following; canvas the property without a search warrant, taking pictures and writing down vehicle information located on the property, deputies was also observed walking to the rear portion of the property, looking into the utility building located in rear of the property, one deputy is observed opening the door of the utility building, one deputy is observed looking into the windows of the utility building, one deputy is observed walking behind the utility building.

As long as the utility building has been located in the rear of the property it has never been locked. This utility building is never locked, never. As deputies were observed returning back to the front of the property, deputies were greeted by the family member inside the home. Once he was noticed by CCSO deputies they became aggressive with him, they started to harass him, they became very disrespectful and rude.

A complaint was made on behalf of these deputies and their actions & behaviors on that day. The home owner called the CCSO several times that morning complaining about the treatment given by the deputies, threatening comments made by the deputies, and the unethical practices of the deputies on that day.

Singling out a dirt bike prompt on the side of the deck, one officer stated "make sure this dirt bike is here when we come back". After several calls made by the homeowner requesting those same officers return to the residence. Complaints ranging from not announcing themselves once they were on the property, the unethical practices seen performed, (deputies were unaware a person was inside the residence plus being seen on surveillance video surrounding the property. Around 1:30 pm the homeowner received a returning call from CCSO, apologizing for the actions & behaviors of the deputies, this call was placed by either Callhaun or Logan. During this conversation she was advised, a detective by the name of Keith and/or Kevin Roberts would be handling this report and he would contact me at a later date to answer any and all questions concerning the incident.

While holding this conversation, the homeowner was asked what would she like to see happen with these officers, it was explained how dangerous it was for the deputies to freely walk around someone else's property, this could have been a very serious issue, someone could of died due to the deputies just felt comfortable to be walk around someone else's property, canvassing the property unlawfully.

The homeowner stated maybe these deputies needed to go back for a refresher course in basic training or maybe they needed an educational course to perform, however the homeowner was merely stating her opinion, bottomline she wanted to express was these deputies unethical practices on that day in May of 2022.

A few days later the homeowner called CCSO in hopes of speaking with the investigating detective at this time it was stated he wasn't available to speak with the homeowner due to having an unexpected emergency. Homeowner was told to return a call the following week. Second attempt the following week, believed to be a Monday morning, the homeowner called CCSO in hopes of speaking with the investigating detective.

During this conversation the homeowner was told this detective wasn't available to speak with her due to an illness. Later within the week the homeowner was contacted by Lt. Callhaun of CCSO, Lt. Callhaun explained there was a search warrant for the utility building on the property, could she come to the residence so they could execute the warrant, he stated "he wanted to know how long it would take for her to get there, he was providing a call because he did not want the same situation to occur as before, it was agree as she headed to the property.

Arriving, the homeowner was introduced to Lt. Mitchell who was now investigating this case. The homeowner asked in reference about what happened with the detective who was originally assigned the case in the beginning. At this time it was stated again, Roberts was out due to an illness. Lt. Callhaun left the property, Lt. Mitchell started to conduct the search of the building. He explained what he was looking for as they were on the property for at least three hours, as he, Lt. Mitchell did not have a positive identification from the victim stating that was indeed indeed his dirt bike.

Lt. Mitchell spoke with Thaxton via facebook messenger. Thaxton was listed as an absconder for probation violation. Lt. Mitchell stated, " I know he (Thaxton) has other things going on with the law but if you could get him on the phone that would be great. Before contacting Thaxton, the homeowner called his daughter's mother to verify she had just purchased a bike for Thaxton.

Receipts for the bike, parts and accessories were provided and shown to Lt. Mitchell while conducting the search. Lt. Mitchell spoke with Thaxton's daughter's mother as well, she stated to Lt. Mitchell, "she purchased the bike and drove to the location to retrieve the bike." Thaxton provided the information of how he obtained such items questioned, provided receipts showing where he purchased the items.

Thaxton was able to provide each person & place where any dealings within reference to any dirt bike located on the property. Observed by others on the property, in our opinion, Lt. Mitchell wasn't concerned with those receipts. Lt. Mitchell was unsure if this was indeed the correct dirt bike, Lt. Mitchell made the decision this was the correct bike due to a special cutting located on the riding seat of the bike. But failed to disclose there were two other seats cut in manner as the one he retrieved. Those seats were present inside the building as well but were not taken in as evidence in the matter.

Investigating Detective Lt. Mitchell, removed a dirt bike from the property still unsure whether or not this was indeed the dirt bike in question of the crime. He stated "if this was found not to be the bike he would return the bike", since this time the bike has been sold. He was improperly investigating the thief of his relatives' property. As stated above, the victim Jayden Mitchell is somehow in relation to Lt. Mitchell by either cousin, father, grandfather, or uncle. As of November 5, 2023 this matter has not been resolved.

Case Number: 23CR225371 & 23CR225372

Felony-POSSESS STOLEN FIREARM Month and Year-January 2023-Caswell County Issues: : Can the police enter your home when you're not there? If somebody is there to let the police in they can request entry by the person who opens the door. The police can enter a house without permission if it is to save or protect a human life in imminent danger (animal life would depend on the type of animal). Otherwise, a search warrant (detailing why the search is necessary) must first be obtained for entry. Failure to do so could deem any evidence found inadmissible.

The argument being evidence may have not been there before the occupier left the house and therefore was constructed by the police. The legal system much prefers the culprit and the evidence to be found together as they then have the uphill struggle of explaining their way out of their predicament.

January 23, 2023-I'm truly not trying to be one of those parents trying to seek justice after the fact- it's my discretion that some of these procedures were unethically conducted by CCSO. Things such as coming on my property without announcing themselves. Those could have been some deadly incidents due to the fact of them not knowing someone was inside the resident and you freely walking around on someone property.

Without permission or any indication of why you're there. My location was 11 miles and 15 mins from 691 Mineral Springs Rd. Tylan picked me up around 2:20-2:30 pm and we returned back around

4:45 pm. I'm positive about this time-I need to confirm an appointment time for the following day, my phone was off and I needed Tylan to make the call to dr to confirm the time.

When he helped me in the house I looked at my calendar where I thought I wrote it down, but I did not. I asked what time it was? We both looked and saw that it was 4:45 pm. I told my son there was still enough time for him to call them for me, get confirmation and to text me back through the wifi. At 5:45 pm, I received a text from Tylan asking me if I could help him pay a bill. I replied to Tylan at 5:53 pm. After this I didn't contact Tylan again until 9:36 pm.

According to the Caswell County news release this happened at 7:30 pm. The timeline is off. This same night the shooter left the scene, came back and shot up the Graves residence thinking it was ours. Proceeded to RDU to catch a flight to LAX the same night. This is basically the baseline for this situation. Both Thaxton's can give more in-depth details from that night. This is the information I have to my knowledge on what happened that night.

These are the events from January 23, 2023. Those detained were K'Shawn Farrish (17), Ace (19) and Sosa (20). Only one I knew to be there is K. Farrish:

So here's the story line from earlier in the day that leads up to 9:36 pm. At 9:36 pm Tylan didn't answer his phone so I called his sister, that call was at 9:38 pm. When I spoke with Talaisha (Tylan) sister I asked her what she was doing, she told me she was in the kitchen washing dishes and they were cleaning up.

So I asked who was there, who were they? Talaisha said it was her, one of my granddaughters and another female, (between ages 15-17). I asked her about two times who was there and she repeated the same. I asked her if the police were there because I received a call that the police were hiding in the woods behind my house.

My daughter advised me there weren't any police at my house at that time. 9:26 pm-I received a call about the Caswell county sheriff dept. Had surrounded my residence 9:36-38 pm- where I stated above where I called my daughter-also during this time after hanging up with my daughter, I called my son to see where he was to tell him about the phone call, I needed him to go to home to check on his sister (she pregnant) 10:30 pm-received a text from my son asking me to call him.

During this call we were trying to figure out what had happened and why the sheriff had my home surrounded. I got off the phone with my son at that time. The next call I received was from my daughter at 11:37 pm.

> 1. 11:37 pm there were deputies at my residence, when I answered the phone, she was yelling, they bum rushed down my driveway to my front door, about 5 to 7 police cars

> 2. During this call I spoke with Chief Foster, I asked him why they were at my residence, he first told me the scent of gunpowder led them to my residence

> 3. He also told me they were looking for 3 individuals involved with a shooting on Mineral Springs. This is when I proceeded to tell him that I was tired of everytime something happens in that area it always has to be my son.

> 4. I told them that I was tired of them coming to my residence for my son. I told him that they shouldn't be at my residence. That my son didn't have anything to do with what had happened.

During this call he advised me that they were going to stay on my property until they received a search warrant, and my reply was it was late and that I was not coming out to give them permission to search my residence. It was later revealed to my son & myself, that an ex-employee of CCSO stated that Durden gave them permission that night to enter my residence-due to the continuous harassment calls being placed by our neighbor Anita Graves. When I visited Durden the following day he aggressively assured me this search was indeed performed correctly.

My daughter repeated every word, so they were aware that I was not coming to give them permission. (the search warrant and permission because an issue with another case, I will explain the comparison at that point). I also stated to him not to get the castings that are already in my yard confused with the casting from this shooting. While being detained she experienced unnecessary roughness (she's pregnant). Also while being detained she explained and expressed how her body was exposed-because there were male officers in her presence and she was naked.

When I mentioned this situation to Durden as a concern-his response was "he didn't care what happened as long as there was a female officer present." My daughter's body was fully uncovered-she had just taken a shower. (per Durden when I mentioned this on the following day he told me that it was none of his concern as long as there was a female officer present during the time. Everyone in my household was detained that night by CCSO.

This shooting involved three individuals I had no knowledge of, by the neighbors calling and reporting my son shot up their home. Which indeed prompted CCSO to my residence once again. Three of the individuals were later found and eventually charged with shooting inside of an occupied dwelling. From the guns in the safe that was located in the residence.

Two weeks later CCSO comes back with warrants for both of the Thaxton twins for felony possession of a stolen firearm. CCSO did a news break with my home-when it was said by neighbors Tylan and the small boys were the one that shot up their house and ran back in the woods towards my residence.

Very very very embarrassing, considering the fact that all parties detained none of which was Tylan. At that moment I wasn't aware that 3 individuals had been found in my residence. It wasn't until the following morning when I canceled my doctor appointment to go to the sheriff office to speak with the Sheriff about the prior night events that's when I found out about the 3 young men. Gunpowder Residue Testing-onsite During the search of the residence CCSO detained 3 individuals, these 3 individuals were considered to be suspects for this shooting.

These 3 individuals that were in custody, they never gave a gun residue testing on the spot vs. when my son was accused of shooting while he was driving, he did admit to firing in the air not at the vehicle. driving on the highway-he was charged cause indeed he had a gun, but he was given the gun residue testing on the spot-Why this wasn't handled in the same fashion in March of 2021? The residence was surrounded with law enforcement, no one administered the gunpowder residue testing.

Per the search warrant they were looking for any and all evidence leading to or associated with shooting into an occupied dwelling. Once receiving the warrant-I was then told by my daughter how the deputies unlawfully entered my residence. As a guest at my residence, there was a 16-17 year old african-american female there who was greeted by a deputy of CCSO- who had already assisted himself to enter my residence w/o executing the search warrant to the homeowner or announcing himself the correct way.

(Through their own admission they stated they didn't want a situation like the last when it came to the search warrant but didn't follow the same protocol this time). The last known disagreement with the Graves that I was aware of around the second to third week of January.

Mr. and Mrs. Graves have had problems with my children before as they have told the deputies on occasion. Mr. and Mrs. Graves said, "it was my son shooting at their residence". They have had disagreements due to the fact of him riding his dirt bike through the path. This elderly couple started calling the police on my son due to him riding his dirt bike-so there's past history. I have also enclosed a copy of my property lines.

They reported shots fired, the report said she was in her bedroom, when I met with the chief and the sheriff the following morning, he stated that, " they were in the living room and bullets went right by their heads". And that she ran and looked out her back door and saw the individuals running TOWARD my residence. One of the MOST IMPORTANT things I mentioned while in their presence, why were they blaming this on my son.

My son wasn't even present, nor was he one of the three detained when they had a news break airing cops surrounding my residence with an active shooter.

May I add two-three hours after the shooting, CCSO said appx. 7:30 pm, time frame isn't correct, this occurred between 6pm-6:45pm. There's an individual that spends a lot of time in my woods located in the back of the residence, this is mainly due to the fact that when I called for patrol about the neighbor that keeps his dogs at his grandmother's home on a piece of my property, no one ever responded to my complaints.

This is how we're able to know about some of the behaviors displayed by CCSO. All of the shooters have been apprehended, none of the three individuals was my son. Tylan DelShaun Thaxton wasn't responsible for the shooting as they were proclaiming because my son and I were together. You have been given all the information I have concerning my complaints against CCSO, RCSO, Reidsville Police Department.

I have mailed copies of this information to the local Law Enforcement Officials CCSO & RCSO and DOJ. Amendment IV Search and arrest-The right of the people to be secure in their persons, houses, papers, and effects, against unreasonable searches and seizures, shall not be violated, and no Warrants shall issue, but upon probable cause, supported by Oath or affirmation, and particularly describing the place to be searched, and the persons or things to be seized.

Amendment VIII Bail, fines, punishment-Excessive bail shall not be required, nor excessive fines imposed, nor cruel and unusual punishments inflicted.

Failure to Intervene-an officer who purposefully allows a fellow officer to violate a victim's constitutional right may be prosecuted for failure to intervene to stop the constitutional violation. To prosecute such an officer, the government must show that the defendant officer was aware of the constitutional violation, had an opportunity to intervene, and chose not to do so.

This charge is often appropriate for supervisory officers who observe uses of excessive force without stopping them or, who actively encourage uses of excessive force but do not directly participate in them.

## **Conflict of Interest-**

Major O. Foster-Major O. Foster-allowed Durden to use excessive tone of voice for almost two minutes as Durden stood up and was very high in tone to get get my house in order and for me to get out of his office

Listening & observing Durden become verbally abusive with me during the conversation, due to me being in disagreement about my son being responsible. He, as I described, became more outrate when I said you were blaming this on my son. Observing how Durden allowed his personal emotions & feelings to become too involved with this case, due to the fact that he was going after the charge of attempted murder of his neighbors.

Observing how Durden's behavior was toward me, his attitude, his temperament, his demeanor, personal feelings, Foster never interrupted, until Durden stood up yelling at me telling me to clean my house and get my house in order, while telling me to get out of his office. I was NOT wanted for questioning. I went to the sheriff department seeking answers about the night before events. I went there to inquire about my residence due to the fact I-We feel like our rights have been violated by CCSO.

I told Durden I would have my son call CCSO with his information he knew about this incident, which my son did. I told Durden I would NOT bring him there for them to arrest him. I'd have him call them and that's what we did. Our actions & behaviors are due to the fact we feel Tylan is a victim of pattern or practice for these law officials in Caswell County.

Due to the strength of our family we're there for one another, as a family if it was NOT for us CCSO would have never caught those shooters especially the one from Reidsville. I feel it's a shame I have to and needed to go through these measurements to protect my son. Due to the rumors of the neighbors, the sheriff & officers of his reputation. When in fact he's only been convicted of one charge.

I truly once again don't want to be another African-American female begging for justice for my son nor burying him at anyone's expense. Tyan was absconded for almost (1) year and a half, Tony Durden stays across the street from us. Sheriff has told me several times before how he's spoken with Tylan about the shooting on our property.

Sheriff has also been to the residence to speak with Tylan about the dirt bikes riding-due to a conflict with the neighbors, (neighbors of us both) for being on their property when indeed it's still my property line that she complains is hers. The point of all this is if Tylan was wanted, he committed all these crimes why was it so hard for law enforcement to get him and he was right across the street the whole entire time.

My son was given a $50k bond due to the reputation Durden upon him-Defamation of Character telling them my son was on felony parole/probation which is isn't, before getting the warrant his judgment was my son doing the shooting-is recommendations of bond caused my son to have this bond amount. As of November 6, 2023 this matter still isn't resolved without an understanding of why.

Provided as well is the statement from one of the individuals detained on January 23, 2023. Today he has been on an electronic monitor since this has occurred, without having the correct understanding of why the monitoring is needed. After several court appearances this still hasn't been resolved. K. Farrish. Sheriff Durden has tried to communicate with Ms. Thaxton, sister, knowing she has an attorney, first being approached during the first appearance, this was reported to her attorney, her attorney stated she needed proof this would be a he say/she say situation.

As you will read the information provided, the methods of communication used by Sheriff Durden in regards of speaking with Ms. Thaxton concerning this situation. More information will be revealed at a later date concerning the rest of this matter being it's still under investigation as well, they all are still under investigation.

Upon the release of this book, there were certain ones who feared for our safety, thank you all from the bottom of our hearts. I have the faith of a mustard seed, any weapons formed against us shall not prosper. With that being said, I fear no man, we fear no man. God is protecting us and he's going to keep making a way out of no way.

For the specific individuals who feel at any time the Britts or Roaches are feeling guilty for their actions with certain loved ones, here's a word of advice, we have no reason to feel guilty about any of the situations God had laid before us. He placed these troubles for a reason; so I La Toye Britt don't have no one thing to feel guilty about concerning any relationships I've endured with my parents and with my children. These writings are for the persons in my life who made the process of learning a need "thing" especially for me, I love to learn and dissect. As most would say, "She knows her parents better than anyone, so Warren Tyree Roach, Sr and

Nina Mae Britt Blackwell, may the both of you sleep in peace. You both have opened the door and it's only up from here.

This is for you both, Love Toy

All rights reserved. No part of this publication is to be reproduced, distributed, or transmitted in any form, means or ways including photocopying. Recording, or any other electronic or mechanical devices, without the prior or proper written permission from the publisher, except in the manner of slight quotations embodied in critical reviews and certain other non commercial uses permitted by copyright law. Any references to historical events, real people, or real places are used non fictitiously. Names, character, and places are real thoughts of the author. Some of the events, names and places have been changed to protect the guilty.

Copyright © 2023 Latoye Britt. August 30, 2024

www.ingramcontent.com/pod-product-compliance
Lightning Source LLC
Chambersburg PA
CBHW052155220526
45471CB00004B/1688